ADVANCED JAVA CONCEPTS

PRACTICAL APPROACH TO IMPLEMENTS CONCEPTS OF JDBC,NETWORKING,MULTITHREADING , SERVLET AND JSP

DR.PRAVIN CHAUDHARI

Made with ♥ on the Notion Press Platform
www.notionpress.com

This book is lovingly dedicated to all aspiring programmers, educators, and mentors who strive to push the boundaries of technology and learning. To my family and friends, thank you for your unwavering support and encouragement throughout this journey and to the readers, may this book inspire and empower you to explore the endless possibilities of advanced Java programming.

Contents

Preface *vii*

1. Java Database Connectivity (JDBC) 1

2. Multithreading In Java 25

3. Java Networking 46

4. Servlet 55

5. JSP (JAVA Server Pages) 85

Preface

In the rapidly evolving world of software development, Java continues to be a cornerstone of innovation and excellence. As one of the most versatile and widely-used programming languages, Java offers an extensive ecosystem for developing robust, scalable, and efficient applications.

This book, Advanced Java Programming: JDBC, Multithreading, and Networking Essentials, is designed for students, professionals, and enthusiasts who want to deepen their understanding of Java's advanced features. It delves into critical topics such as database connectivity (JDBC), multithreading, networking, and server-side programming with servlets. Each concept is illustrated with practical examples, enabling readers to bridge the gap between theory and real-world application.

The book is structured to facilitate both guided learning and self-paced exploration. Starting with Java Database Connectivity (JDBC), it covers the principles of interacting with relational databases, followed by multithreading concepts to harness the power of parallel processing. Networking fundamentals are explored to enable seamless communication between systems, and finally, servlets are introduced to build dynamic, web-based applications.

The goal of this book is not only to impart technical knowledge but also to encourage readers to think creatively and build innovative solutions using Java. Whether you are a student eager to master advanced programming techniques or a professional aiming to enhance your skill set, this book provides a comprehensive guide to excel in Java development.

We hope this book becomes a valuable resource in your journey as a Java programmer. Thank you for choosing to embark on this learning experience with us.

Warm regards,
[Dr.Pravin Chaudhari]

CHAPTER I

Java Database Connectivity (JDBC)

Introduction to JDBC

Java Database Connectivity (JDBC) is an Application Programming Interface(API) used to connect Java application with Database. JDBC is used to interact with various type of Database such as Oracle, MS Access, My SQL and SQL Server. JDBC can also be defined as the platform-independent interface between a relational database and Java programming. It allows java program to execute SQL statement and retrieve result from database.

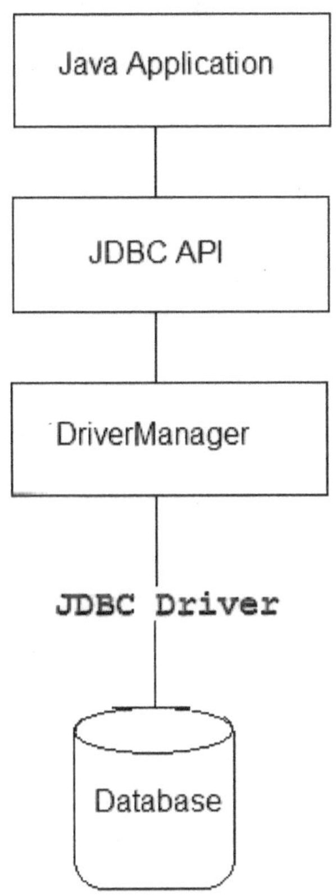

Fig. Architecture of JDBC

JDBC is new and advance specification of JDBC. It provides the following advance features

- Connection Management
- Auto loading of Driver Interface.
- Better exception handling
- Support for large object
- Annotation in SQL query.

JDBC Driver

JDBC Driver is required to process SQL requests and generate result. The following are the different types of driver available in JDBC.

Type-1 Driver or JDBC-ODBC bridge

Type-2 Driver or Native API Partly Java Driver

Type-3 Driver or Network Protocol Driver

Type-4 Driver or Thin Driver

JDBC-ODBC bridge

Type-1 Driver act as a bridge between JDBC and other database connectivity mechanism (ODBC). This driver converts JDBC calls into ODBC calls and redirects the request to the ODBC driver.

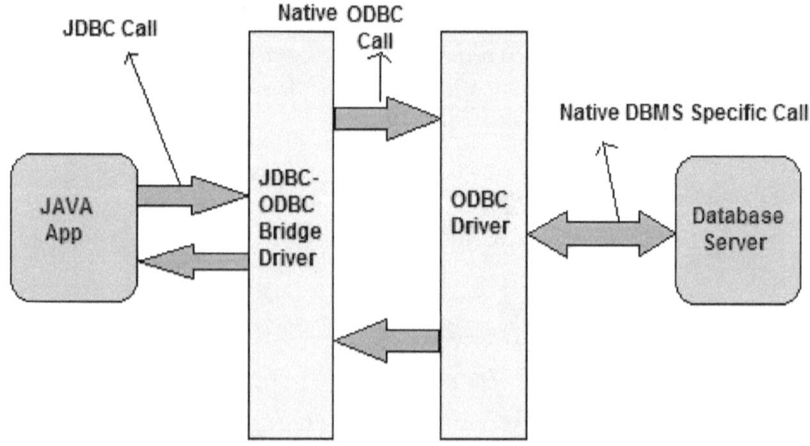

Type-1 Driver - JDBC ODBC Bridge

Advantages:

- Easy to use
- Allow easy connectivity to all database supported by the ODBC Driver .

Disadvantage:

- Slow execution time
- Dependent on ODBC Driver.
- Uses Java Native Interface(JNI) to make ODBC call.

Native API Driver

This type of driver make use of Java Native Interface(JNI) call on database specific native client API. These native client API are usually written in C and C++.

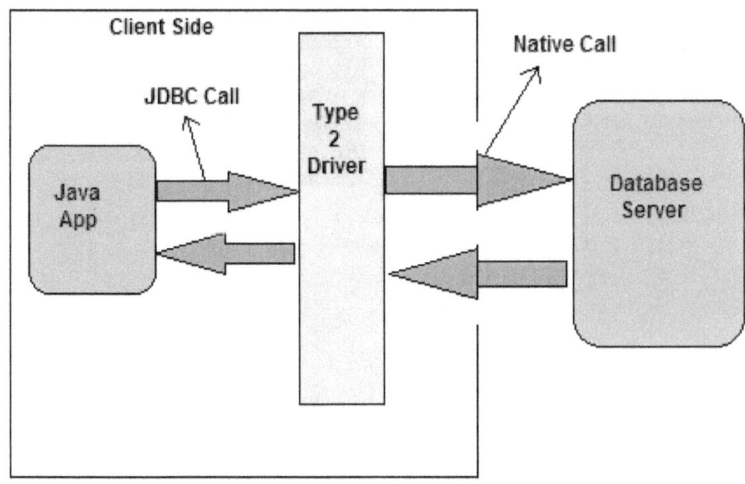

Type-2 Driver -Native API

Advantages:

- faster as compared to Type-1 Driver
- Contains additional features.

Disadvantages

- Requires native library
- Increased cost of Application

Network Protocol Driver

This driver translate the JDBC calls into a database server independent and Middleware server-specific calls. Middleware server further translate JDBC calls into database specific calls.

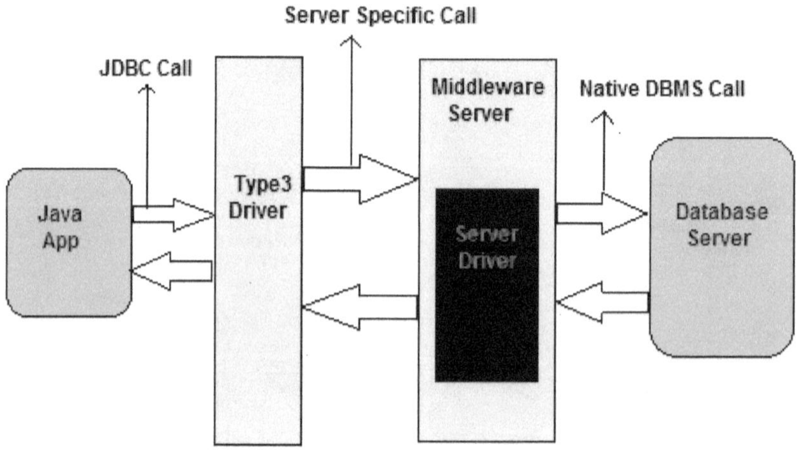

Type 3 Driver-Network Protocol

Advantages:

- Does not require any native library to be installed.
- Database Independency.
- Provide facility to switch over from one database to another database.

Disadvantage:

- Slow due to increase number of network call.

Thin Driver

This is Driver called Pure Java Driver because. This driver interacts directly with database. It does not require any native database library, that is why it is also known as Thin Driver.

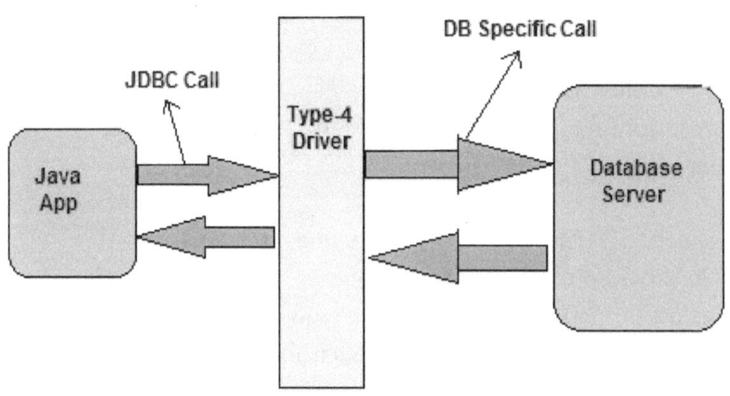

Type 4 Driver- Thin Driver

Advantages:

- Does not require any native library.
- Does not require any Middleware server.
- Better Performance than another driver.

Disadvantages:

- Slow due to increase number of network call.

Steps to connect a Java Application to Database

The following 5 steps are the basic steps involve in connecting a Java application with Database using JDBC.

1. Driver Registration
2. Creation of Connection
3. Creation Statement
4. Execute SQL Queries and Create Object of ReultSet.
5. Close connection.

Driver Registration

Class.forName() is used to load the driver class explicitly.

Example to register with JDBC-ODBC Driver

Class.forName("oracle.jdbc.driver.OracleDriver");

Create a Connection

getConnection() method of DriverManager class is used to create a connection.

Syntax

getConnection(String url, String username, String password)

Example establish connection with Oracle

Connection con = DriverManager.getConnection("jdbc:oracle:thin:@localhost:1521:xe", "system","root");

Create Statement

createStatement() method is invoked on current Connection object to create a SQL Statement.

Syntax

public Statement createStatement() throws SQLException

Example to create a SQL statement

Statement s=con.createStatement();

Execute SQL Queries and Create ResultSet

executeQuery() method of Statement interface is used to execute SQL statements.

Syntax

public ResultSet executeQuery(String query) throws SQLException

Example to execute a SQL statement

```
ResultSet rs=s.executeQuery("select * from student"); // student( rollno, name)
while(rs.next())
{
System.out.println(rs.getInt(1)+" "+rs.getString(2));
}
```

Closing the connection

After executing SQL statement you need to close the connection and release the session. The close() method of Connection interface is used to close the connection.

Syntax

public void close() throws SQLException

Example of closing a connection

con.close();

Connecting to oracle Database

Example:-

We suppose that you have created a student table with rollno and name column name in oracle database.

```
import java.sql.*;
class StudentDemo
{
public static void main(String []args)
{
try{
Class.forName("oracle.jdbc.driver.OracleDriver");
Connection con =
DriverManager.getConnection("jdbc:oracle:thin:@localhost:1521:xe",
"system","root");
Statement s=con.createStatement(); //creating statement
ResultSet rs=s.executeQuery("select * from student"); //executing
statement
while(rs.next()){
System.out.println(rs.getInt(1)+" "+rs.getString(2));
}
con.close(); //closing connection
}
catch(Exception e)
{
e.printStackTrace();
}
}
}
```

DriverManager class

The DriverManager class acts as an interface between user and drivers. It keeps track of the drivers that are available and handles establishing a connection between a database and the appropriate driver. The DriverManager class maintains a list of Driver classes that have registered themselves by calling the method DriverManager.registerDriver().

Useful methods of DriverManager class

Method

1) public static Connection getConnection(String url):

is used to establish the connection with the specified url.

2) public static Connection getConnection(String url,String userName,String password):

is used to establish the connection with the specified url, username and password.

Connection interface

A Connection is the session between java application and database. The Connection interface is a factory of Statement, PreparedStatement, and DatabaseMetaData i.e. object of Connection can be used to get the object of Statement and DatabaseMetaData. The Connection interface provide many methods for transaction management like commit (), rollback () etc.

Commonly used methods of Connection interface:

1) public Statement createStatement(): creates a statement object that can be used to execute SQL queries.

2) public Statement createStatement(int resultSetType,int resultSetConcurrency): Creates a Statement object that will generate ResultSet objects with the given type and concurrency.

3) public void setAutoCommit(boolean status): is used to set the commit status.By default it is true.

4) public void commit(): saves the changes made since the previous commit/rollback permanent.

5) public void rollback(): Drops all changes made since the previous commit/rollback.

6) public void close(): closes the connection and Releases a JDBC resources immediately.

Statement interface

The Statement interface provides methods to execute queries with the database. The statement interface is a factory of ResultSet i.e. it provides factory method to get the object of ResultSet.

Commonly used methods of Statement interface:

The important methods of Statement interface are as follows:

1) public ResultSet executeQuery(String sql): is used to execute SELECT query. It returns the object of ResultSet.

2) public int executeUpdate(String sql): is used to execute specified query, it may be create, drop, insert, update, delete etc.

3) public boolean execute(String sql): is used to execute queries that may return multiple results.

4) public int[] executeBatch(): is used to execute batch of commands.

Example of Statement interface

Let's see the simple example of Statement interface to insert, update and delete the record.

```
import java.sql.*;
class InsertRecord{
public static void main(String args[])throws Exception{
Class.forName("oracle.jdbc.driver.OracleDriver");
Connection con==
DriverManager.getConnection("jdbc:oracle:thin:@localhost:1521:xe",
"system","root");
Statement stmt=con.createStatement();
stmt. executeUpdate("insert into employee values(10,'pravin',5000)");
int r=stmt.executeUpdate("update employee set
name='ABC',salary=10000 where id=10");
int r=stmt.executeUpdate("delete from employee where id=10");
System.out.println(r+" records affected");
con.close();
}
}
```

ResultSet interface

The object of ResultSet maintains a cursor pointing to a row of a table. Initially, cursor points to before the first row.

By default, ResultSet object can be moved forward only and it is not updatable.

Commonly used methods of ResultSet interface

1) public boolean next():

is used to move the cursor to the one row next from the current position.

2) public boolean previous():

is used to move the cursor to the one row previous from the current position.

3) public boolean first():

is used to move the cursor to the first row in result set object.

4) public boolean last():

is used to move the cursor to the last row in result set object.

5) public boolean absolute(int row):

is used to move the cursor to the specified row number in the ResultSet object.

6) public int getInt(int columnIndex):

is used to return the data of specified column index of the current row as int.

7) public int getInt(String columnName):

is used to return the data of specified column name of the current row as int.

8) public String getString(int columnIndex):

is used to return the data of specified column index of the current row as String.

9) public String getString(String columnName):

is used to return the data of specified column name of the current row as String.

Making ResultSet Scrollable:-

We can make ResultSet Scrollable (move cursor forward and backward direction) by passing two parameters in createStatement() method.

First Parameter is either TYPE_SCROLL_FORWARD_ONLY or TYPE_SCROLL_INSENSITIVE or TYPE_SCROLL_SENSITIVE and second parameter either CONCUR_READ_ONLY or CONCUR_UPDATABLE in createStatement(int,int) method

Systntx:-

```
Statement stmt = con.
createStatement(ResultSet.TYPE_SCROLL_INSENSITIVE,
ResultSet.CONCUR_UPDATABLE);
```

Example of Scrollable ResultSet

```
import java.sql.*;
class ResultSetDemo{
publicstaticvoid main(String args[])throws Exception{
Class.forName("oracle.jdbc.driver.OracleDriver");
Connection con==
DriverManager.getConnection("jdbc:oracle:thin:@localhost:1521:xe",
"system","root");
```

```
Statement
stmt=con.createStatement(ResultSet.TYPE_SCROLL_SENSITIVE,
ResultSet.CONCUR_UPDATABLE);
ResultSet rs=stmt.executeQuery("select * from student");
rs.next();
System.out.println(rs.getInt(1)+" "+rs.getString(2));
rs.last();
System.out.println(rs.getInt(1)+" "+rs.getString(2));
rs.previous();
System.out.println(rs.getInt(1)+" "+rs.getString(2));
rs.first();
System.out.println(rs.getInt(1)+" "+rs.getString(2));
con.close();
}
}
```

Types of Statement

1.Statement

con.createStatement()

2.PreparedStatement

con.prepareStatement(Query);

3.CallableStatement

to call strored Procedure/function from database

public CallableStatement con.prepareCall("{ call procedurename(?,?...?)}");

CallableStatement cs=con.prepareCall("{ call p1(tno,tname,sal,design)}");

PreparedStatement interface

The PreparedStatement interface is a sub interface of Statement. It is used to execute parameterized query.

Let's see the example of parameterized query:

String sql="insert into emp values(?,?,?)";

As you can see, we are passing parameter (?) for the values. Its value will be set by calling the setter methods of PreparedStatement.

Why use PreparedStatement?

Improves performance: The performance of the application will be faster if you use PreparedStatement interface because query is compiled only once.

How to get the instance of PreparedStatement?

The prepareStatement() method of Connection interface is used to return the object of PreparedStatement.

Syntax:

public PreparedStatement prepareStatement(String query)**throws** SQLException{}

Methods of PreparedStatement interface

- public void setInt(int paramIndex, int value) sets the integer value to the given parameter index.
- public void setString(int paramIndex, String value)sets the String value to the given parameter index.
- public void setFloat(int paramIndex, float value)sets the float value to the given parameter index.
- public void setDouble(int paramIndex, double value)sets the double value to the given parameter index.
- public int executeUpdate()executes the query. It is used for create, drop, insert, update, delete etc.
- public ResultSet executeQuery()executes the select query. It returns an instance of ResultSet.

Example of PreparedStatement interface that inserts the record

First of all create table as given below:

create table employee(id number(10),name varchar2(50));

Now insert records in this table by the code given below:

```
import java.sql.*;
class InsertPrepared{
publicstaticvoid main(String args[]){
try{
Class.forName("oracle.jdbc.driver.OracleDriver");
Connection con==
DriverManager.getConnection("jdbc:oracle:thin:@localhost:1521:xe",
"system","root");
PreparedStatement stmt=con.prepareStatement("insert into employee
values(?,?)");
stmt.setInt(1,101);//1 specifies the first parameter in the query
stmt.setString(2,"pravin");
int i=stmt.executeUpdate();
System.out.println(i+" records inserted");
```

```
con.close();
}catch(Exception e){ System.out.println(e);}
}
}
```

Example of PreparedStatement interface that updates the record

```
PreparedStatement stmt=con.prepareStatement("update employee set name=? where id=?");
stmt.setString(1,"XYZ");//1 specifies the first parameter in the query i.e. name
stmt.setInt(2,101);
int i=stmt.executeUpdate();
System.out.println(i+" records updated");
```

Example of PreparedStatement interface that deletes the record

```
PreparedStatement stmt=con.prepareStatement("delete from employee where id=?");
stmt.setInt(1,101);
int i=stmt.executeUpdate();
System.out.println(i+" records deleted");
```

Example of PreparedStatement interface that retrieve the records of a table

```
PreparedStatement stmt=con.prepareStatement("select * from employee");
ResultSet rs=stmt.executeQuery();
while(rs.next()){
System.out.println(rs.getInt(1)+" "+rs.getString(2));
}
```

Java ResultSetMetaData Interface

The metadata means data about data i.e. we can get further information from the data.

If you have to get metadata of a table like total number of column, column name, column type etc. , ResultSetMetaData interface is useful because it provides methods to get metadata from the ResultSet object.

Commonly used methods of ResultSetMetaData interface

Method

- public int getColumnCount()throws SQLExceptionit returns the total number of columns in the ResultSet object.

- public String getColumnName(int index)throws SQLExceptionit returns the column name of the specified column index.
- public String getColumnTypeName(int index)throws SQLExceptionit returns the column type name for the specified index.
- public String getTableName(int index)throws SQLExceptionit returns the table name for the specified column index.

How to get the object of ResultSetMetaData:

The getMetaData() method of ResultSet interface returns the object of ResultSetMetaData. Syntax:

```
public ResultSetMetaData getMetaData()throws SQLException
```

Example of ResultSetMetaData interface :

```
import java.sql.*;
class Rsmd{
publicstaticvoid main(String args[]){
try{
Class.forName("oracle.jdbc.driver.OracleDriver");
Connection con=
DriverManager.getConnection("jdbc:oracle:thin:@localhost:1521:xe",
"system","root");
PreparedStatement ps=con.prepareStatement("select * from employee");
ResultSet rs=ps.executeQuery();
ResultSetMetaData rsmd=rs.getMetaData();
System.out.println("Total columns: "+rsmd.getColumnCount());
System.out.println("Column Name of 1st column: "+rsmd.getColumnName(1));
System.out.println("Column Type Name of 1st column: "+rsmd.getColumnTypeName(1));
con.close();
}catch(Exception e)
{ System.out.println(e);
}
}
}
```

Java DatabaseMetaData interface

DatabaseMetaData interface provides methods to get meta data of a database such as database product name, database product version, driver name, name of total number of tables, name of total number of views etc.

Commonly used methods of DatabaseMetaData interface

1. public String getDriverName()throws SQLException: it returns the name of the JDBC driver.
2. public String getDriverVersion()throws SQLException: it returns the version number of the JDBC driver.
3. public String getUserName()throws SQLException: it returns the username of the database.
4. public String getDatabaseProductName()throws SQLException: it returns the product name of the database.
5. public String getDatabaseProductVersion()throws SQLException: it returns the product version of the database.
6. public ResultSet getTables(String catalog, String schemaPattern, String tableNamePattern, String[] types)throws SQLException: it returns the description of the tables of the specified catalog. The table type can be TABLE, VIEW, ALIAS, SYSTEM TABLE, SYNONYM etc.

How to get the object of DatabaseMetaData:

The getMetaData() method of Connection interface returns the object of DatabaseMetaData.

Syntax:

public DatabaseMetaData getMetaData()throws SQLException

Simple Example of DatabaseMetaData interface :

```
import java.sql.*;
class DBMD1{
public static void main(String args[]){
try{
Class.forName("oracle.jdbc.driver.OracleDriver");
Connection con==
DriverManager.getConnection("jdbc:oracle:thin:@localhost:1521:xe",
"system","root");
DatabaseMetaData dbmd=con.getMetaData();
System.out.println("Driver Name: "+dbmd.getDriverName());
System.out.println("Driver Version: "+dbmd.getDriverVersion());
System.out.println("UserName: "+dbmd.getUserName());
System.out.println("Database Product Name:
"+dbmd.getDatabaseProductName());
```

```
System.out.println("Database Product Version: "+dbmd.getDatabaseProductVersion());
con.close();
}catch(Exception e){ System.out.println(e);}
}
}
```

Example of DatabaseMetaData interface that prints total number of tables in database :

```
import java.sql.*;
class DBMD2{
public static void main(String args[]){
try{
Class.forName("oracle.jdbc.driver.OracleDriver");
Connection con== DriverManager.getConnection("jdbc:oracle:thin:@localhost:1521:xe",
"system","root");
DatabaseMetaData dbmd=con.getMetaData();
String table[]={"TABLE"};
ResultSet rs=dbmd.getTables(null,null,null,table);
while(rs.next()){
System.out.println(rs.getString(3));
}
con.close();
}catch(Exception e){ System.out.println(e);}
}
}
```

More Practice Programs on JDBC:

1.Write a menu driven program in Java for the following: Assume Emp table with attributes (ENo, EName, salary, Desg) is already created.

1. Insert
2. Update
3. Delete
4. Search
5. Display
6. Exit.

```
import java.sql.*;
import java.util.*;
public class JDBCOperation{
```

```
public static void main(String[] args) throws Exception {
Class.forName("oracle.jdbc.driver.OracleDriver");
Connection
con=DriverManager.getConnection("jdbc:oracle:thin:@localhost:1521:xe",
"system","root");
Statement st = con.createStatement();
Scanner sc = new Scanner(System.in);
while (true) {
System.out.println("\n1. Insert\n2. Update\n3. Delete\n4. Search\n5.
Display\n6. Exit");
System.out.println("Enter Your Option");
int opt = sc.nextInt();
switch (opt) {
case 1:
System.out.println("Enter eno, ename and salary");
int e = sc.nextInt();
String n = sc.next();
int sal = sc.nextInt();
st.executeUpdate("Insert into emp values (" + e + ", ‘" + n + "’, " + sal +
")");
System.out.println("Record Inserted");
break;
case 2:
System.out.println("Enter eno, ename and salary");
e = sc.nextInt();
n = sc.next();
sal = sc.nextInt();
st.executeUpdate("update emp set ename = ‘" + n +"’, sal = " + sal + "
where eno = " + e+"");
System.out.println("Record Updated");
break;
case 3:
System.out.println("Enter eno to delete record");
e = sc.nextInt();
st.executeUpdate("delete from emp where eno = " + e);
System.out.println("Record Deleted");
break;
case 4:
```

```
System.out.println("Enter eno to Search Record");
e = sc.nextInt();
ResultSet rs = st.executeQuery("Select * from emp where eno = " + e);
while (rs.next()) {
System.out.print("\t" + rs.getInt(1));
System.out.print("\t" + rs.getString(2));
System.out.print("\t" + rs.getInt(3));
System.out.println("\n");
}
break;
case 5:
rs = st.executeQuery("select * from emp");
while (rs.next()) {
System.out.print("" + rs.getInt(1));
System.out.print("" + rs.getString(2));
System.out.print("" + rs.getInt(3));
}
break;
case 6:
System.exit(0);
}
}
}
}
```

2. Write a java program to count the number of records in a table

```
import java.sql.Connection;
import java.sql.DriverManager;
import java.sql.ResultSet;
import java.sql.Statement;
public class JDBCCount {
public static void main(String[] args) throws Exception
{
// TODO Auto-generated method stub
Class.forName("oracle.jdbc.driver.OracleDriver");
Connection
con=DriverManager.getConnection("jdbc:oracle:thin:@localhost:1521:xe",
"system","root");
Statement st=con.createStatement();
```

```
ResultSet rs=st.executeQuery("select * from student");
int c=0;
while(rs.next())
{
c++;
}
System.out.println("No. of records="+ c);
}
}
```

3. Write a Java Program to delete details of students whose initial character of their namc is 'S'.

```
import java.sql.Connection;
import java.sql.DriverManager;
import java.sql.ResultSet;
import java.sql.Statement;
public class JDBCDelete {
public static void main(String[] args) throws Exception
{
// TODO Auto-generated method stub
Class.forName("oracle.jdbc.driver.OracleDriver");
Connection
con=DriverManager.getConnection("jdbc:oracle:thin:@localhost:1521:xe",
"system","root");
Statement st=con.createStatement();
st.executeUpdate("delete from student whcrc sname like 's%'");
System.out.println("Record Deleted");
}
}
```

4. Write a Java program to accept the details of students (rno, sname, per) at least 5 Records,

store it into database and display the details of student having highest percentage.

(Use PreparedStatement Interface)

```
import java.sql.*;
import java.sql.DriverManager;
import java.sql.ResultSet;
import java.sql.Statement;
public class DisplayMaxPer {
```

```
public static void main(String[] args) throws Exception {
// TODO Auto-generated method stub
Class.forName("oracle.jdbc.driver.OracleDriver");
Connection
con=DriverManager.getConnection("jdbc:oracle:thin:@localhost:1521:xe",
"system","root");
PreparedStatement st=con.prepareStatement("select * from student
where per=
(select max(per) from student)");
ResultSet rs=st.executeQuery();
while(rs.next())
{
System.out.println(""+rs.getInt(1)+"\t"+rs.getString(2)+"\t"+rs.getInt(3));
}
con.close();
}
}
```

5. Java Swing-based application that allows you to perform CRUD (Create, Read, Update, Delete) operations on a student table in an Oracle database. This application connects to the database and provides a graphical user interface (GUI) to interact with the student table.

```
import javax.swing.*;
import java.awt.*;
import java.awt.event.*;
import java.sql.*;
public class StudentApp {
private JFrame frame;
private JTextField txtId, txtName, txtAge, txtGrade;
private JTextArea outputArea;
private Connection con;
public StudentApp() {
frame = new JFrame("Student Management Application");
frame.setDefaultCloseOperation(JFrame.EXIT_ON_CLOSE);
frame.setSize(600, 500);
JPanel panel = new JPanel(new GridLayout(6, 2));
panel.add(new JLabel("ID:"));
txtId = new JTextField();
panel.add(txtId);
```

```
panel.add(new JLabel("Name:"));
txtName = new JTextField();
panel.add(txtName);
panel.add(new JLabel("Age:"));
txtAge = new JTextField();
panel.add(txtAge);
panel.add(new JLabel("Grade:"));
txtGrade = new JTextField();
panel.add(txtGrade);
JButton btnInsert = new JButton("Insert");
btnInsert.addActionListener(e -> insertStudent());
panel.add(btnInsert);
JButton btnUpdate = new JButton("Update");
btnUpdate.addActionListener(e -> updateStudent());
panel.add(btnUpdate);
JButton btnDelete = new JButton("Delete");
btnDelete.addActionListener(e -> deleteStudent());
panel.add(btnDelete);
JButton btnSearch = new JButton("Search");
btnSearch.addActionListener(e -> searchStudent());
panel.add(btnSearch);
JButton btnViewAll = new JButton("View All");
btnViewAll.addActionListener(e -> viewAllStudents());
panel.add(btnViewAll);
frame.add(panel, BorderLayout.NORTH);
outputArea = new JTextArea();
outputArea.setEditable(false);
frame.add(new JScrollPane(outputArea), BorderLayout.CENTER);
frame.setVisible(true);
try
{
Class.forName("oracle.jdbc.driver.OracleDriver");
con=DriverManager.getConnection("jdbc:oracle:thin:@localhost:1521:xe",
"system","root");
}
catch(Exception e) {}
}
private void insertStudent() {
```

```
try {
PreparedStatement pst = con.prepareStatement("INSERT INTO student
VALUES (?, ?, ?, ?)");
pst.setInt(1, Integer.parseInt(txtId.getText()));
pst.setString(2, txtName.getText());
pst.setInt(3, Integer.parseInt(txtAge.getText()));
pst.setString(4, txtGrade.getText());
int rows = pst.executeUpdate();
outputArea.setText(rows + " student(s) inserted.");
} catch (Exception ex) {
outputArea.setText("Error: " + ex.getMessage());
}
}
private void updateStudent() {
try {
PreparedStatement pst = con.prepareStatement("UPDATE student SET
name = ?, age = ?
, grade = ? WHERE id = ?");
pst.setString(1, txtName.getText());
pst.setInt(2, Integer.parseInt(txtAge.getText()));
pst.setString(3, txtGrade.getText());
pst.setInt(4, Integer.parseInt(txtId.getText()));
int rows = pst.executeUpdate();
outputArea.setText(rows + " student(s) updated.");
} catch (Exception ex) {
outputArea.setText("Error: " + ex.getMessage());
}
}
private void deleteStudent() {
try {
PreparedStatement pst = con.prepareStatement("DELETE FROM
student WHERE id = ?");
pst.setInt(1, Integer.parseInt(txtId.getText()));
int rows = pst.executeUpdate();
outputArea.setText(rows + " student(s) deleted.");
} catch (Exception ex) {
outputArea.setText("Error: " + ex.getMessage());
}
```

```
}
private void searchStudent() {
try {
PreparedStatement pst = con.prepareStatement("SELECT * FROM
student WHERE id = ?");
pst.setInt(1, Integer.parseInt(txtId.getText()));
try (ResultSet rs = pst.executeQuery()) {
if (rs.next()) {
outputArea.setText("ID: " + rs.getInt("id") + "\n" +
"Name: " + rs.getString("name") + "\n" +
"Age: " + rs.getInt("age") + "\n" +
"Grade: " + rs.getString("grade"));
} else {
outputArea.setText("No student found with ID " + txtId.getText());
}
}
} catch (Exception ex) {
outputArea.setText("Error: " + ex.getMessage());
}
}
private void viewAllStudents() {
try {
Statement stmt = con.createStatement();
ResultSet rs = stmt.executeQuery("SELECT * FROM student");
StringBuilder sb = new StringBuilder();
while (rs.next()) {
sb.append("ID: ").append(rs.getInt("id"))
.append(", Name: ").append(rs.getString("name"))
.append(", Age: ").append(rs.getInt("age"))
.append(", Grade: ").append(rs.getString("grade"))
.append("\n");
}
outputArea.setText(sb.toString());
} catch (Exception ex) {
outputArea.setText("Error: " + ex.getMessage());
}
}
public static void main(String[] args) {
```

```
SwingUtilities.invokeLater(StudentApp::new);
}
}
```

CHAPTER II

Multithreading in Java

Important Concept:

Multithreading

Multitasking

Process-based multitasking

Thread-based multitasking

What is Thread

Multithreading in Java is a process of executing multiple threads simultaneously.

A thread is a lightweight sub-process, the smallest unit of processing. Multiprocessing and multithreading, both are used to achieve multitasking.

However, we use multithreading than multiprocessing because threads use a shared memory area. They don't allocate separate memory area so saves memory, and context-switching between the threads takes less time than process.

Java Multithreading is mostly used in games, animation, etc.

Advantages of Java Multithreading

1) It **doesn't block the user** because threads are independent and you can perform multiple operations at the same time.

2) You **can perform many operations together, so it saves time**.

3) Threads are **independent**, so it doesn't affect other threads if an exception occurs in a single thread.

Multitasking

Multitasking is a process of executing multiple tasks simultaneously. We use multitasking to utilize the CPU. Multitasking can be achieved in two ways:

Process-based Multitasking (Multiprocessing)

Thread-based Multitasking (Multithreading)

1) Process-based Multitasking (Multiprocessing)

Each process has an address in memory. In other words, each process allocates a separate memory area.

A process is heavyweight.

Cost of communication between the process is high.

Switching from one process to another requires some time for saving and loading registers, memory maps, updating lists, etc.

2) Thread-based Multitasking (Multithreading)

Threads share the same address space.

A thread is lightweight.

Cost of communication between the thread is low.

Note: At least one process is required for each thread.

What is Thread in java

A thread is a lightweight subprocess, the smallest unit of processing. It is a separate path of execution.

Threads are independent. If there occurs exception in one thread, it doesn't affect other threads. It uses a shared memory area.

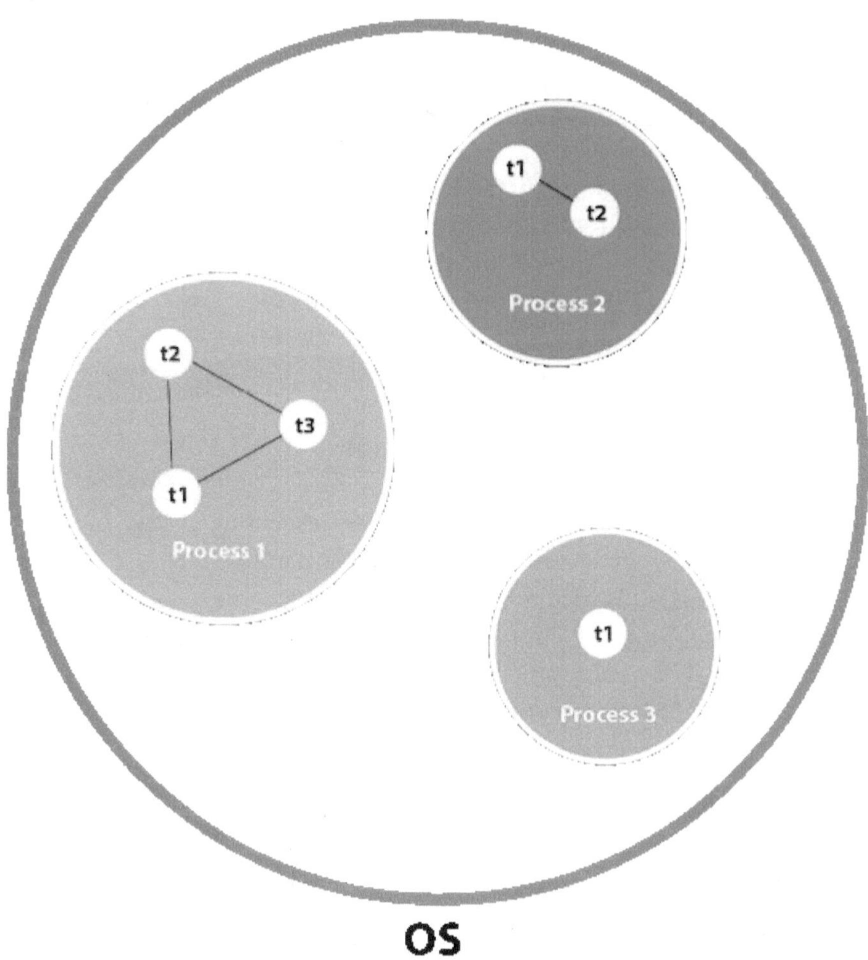

Structure of Thread in OS

As shown in the above figure, a thread is executed inside the process. There is context-switching between the threads. There can be multiple processes inside the OS, and one process can have multiple threads.

Java Thread class

Java provides **Thread class** to achieve thread programming. Thread class provides constructors and methods to create and perform operations on a thread. Thread class extends Object class and implements Runnable interface.

Java Thread Methods

- void start()-It is used to start the execution of the thread.
- void run() -It is used to do an action for a thread.
- static void sleep()-It sleeps a thread for the specified amount of time.
- static Thread currentThread()-It returns a reference to the currently executing thread object.
- void join() -It waits for a thread to die.
- int getPriority() -It returns the priority of the thread.
- void setPriority()-It changes the priority of the thread.
- String getName()-It returns the name of the thread.
- void setName()-It changes the name of the thread.
- long getId()-It returns the id of the thread.

boolean isAlive()-It tests if the thread is alive.

- static void yield()-It causes the currently executing thread object to pause and allow other threads to execute temporarily.
- void suspend()-It is used to suspend the thread.
- void resume()-It is used to resume the suspended thread.
- void stop()-It is used to stop the thread.
- void destroy()-It is used to destroy the thread group and all of its subgroups.
- String toString() It is used to return a string representation of this thread, including the thread's name, priority, and thread group.
- void notify() -It is used to give the notification for only one thread which is waiting for a particular object.
- void notifyAll()-It is used to give the notification to all waiting threads of a particular object.

Life cycle of a Thread (Thread States)

A thread can be in one of the five states. According to sun, there is only 4 states in thread life cycle in java new, runnable, non-runnable and terminated. There is no running state.

But for better understanding the threads, we are explaining it in the 5 states.

The life cycle of the thread in java is controlled by JVM. The java thread states are as follows:

- New

- Runnable
- Running
- Non-Runnable (Blocked)
- Terminated

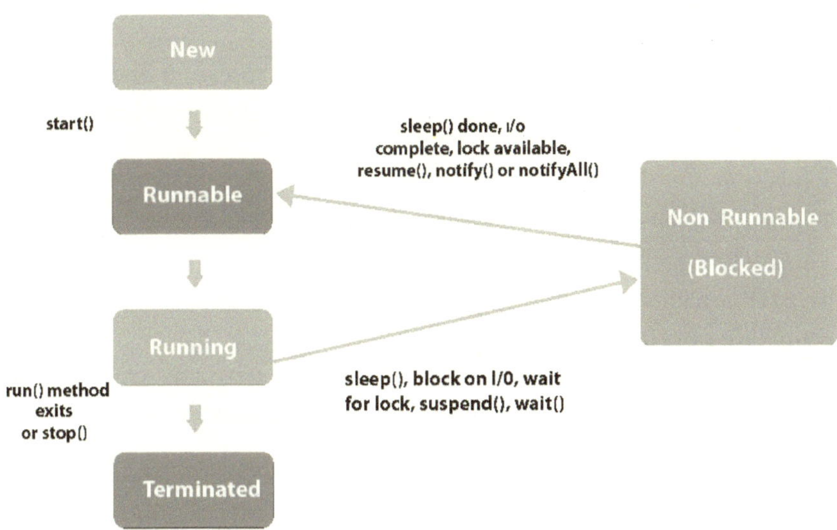

Life Cycle of Thread

1) New

The thread is in new state if you create an instance of Thread class but before the invocation of start() method.

2) Runnable

The thread is in runnable state after invocation of start() method, but the thread scheduler has not selected it to be the running thread.

3) Running

The thread is in running state if the thread scheduler has selected it.

4) Non-Runnable (Blocked)

This is the state when the thread is still alive, but is currently not eligible to run.

5) Terminated

A thread is in terminated or dead state when its run() method exits.

How to create thread

There are two ways to create a thread:

1. By extending Thread class
2. By implementing Runnable interface.

Thread class:

Commonly used Constructors of Thread class:

Thread class provide constructors and methods to create and perform operations on a thread.Thread class extends Object class and implements Runnable interface.

Thread()

Thread(String name)

Thread(Runnable r)

hread(Runnable r,String name)

Runnable interface:

The Runnable interface should be implemented by any class whose instances are intended to be executed by a thread. Runnable interface have only one method named run().

public void run(): is used to perform action for a thread.

Starting a thread:

start() method of Thread class is used to start a newly created thread. It performs following tasks:

A new thread starts(with new callstack).

The thread moves from New state to the Runnable state.

When the thread gets a chance to execute, its target run() method will run.

1) Java Thread Example by extending Thread class

```
class Multi extends Thread{
public void run(){
System.out.println("thread is running...");
}
public static void main(String args[]){
Multi t1=new Multi();
t1.start();
}
}
```

2) Java Thread Example by implementing Runnable interface

```
class Multi3 implements Runnable{
public void run(){
System.out.println("thread is running...");
}
public static void main(String args[]){
Multi3 m1=new Multi3();
Thread t1 =new Thread(m1);
t1.start();
}
}
```

If you are not extending the Thread class,your class object would not be treated as a thread object.So you need to explicitely create Thread class object.We are passing the object of your class that implements Runnable so that your class run() method may execute.

Sleep method in java

The sleep() method of Thread class is used to sleep a thread for the specified amount of time.

Syntax of sleep() method in java

The Thread class provides two methods for sleeping a thread:

public static void sleep(long miliseconds)throws InterruptedException

public static void sleep(long miliseconds, int nanos)throws InterruptedException

Example of sleep method in java

```
class TestSleepMethod1 extends Thread{
public void run(){
for(int i=1;i<5;i++){
try{Thread.sleep(500);}catch(InterruptedException
e){System.out.println(e);}
System.out.println(i);
}
}
public static void main(String args[]){
TestSleepMethod1 t1=new TestSleepMethod1();
TestSleepMethod1 t2=new TestSleepMethod1();
t1.start();
t2.start();
}
}
```

Priority of a Thread (Thread Priority):

Each thread have a priority. Priorities are represented by a number between 1 and 10. In most cases, thread schedular schedules the threads according to their priority (known as preemptive scheduling). But it is not guaranteed because it depends on JVM specification that which scheduling it chooses.

constants defined in Thread class:

- public static int MIN_PRIORITY
- public static int NORM_PRIORITY
- public static int MAX_PRIORITY

Default priority of a thread is 5 (NORM_PRIORITY). The value of MIN_PRIORITY is 1 and the value of MAX_PRIORITY is 10.

Example of priority of a Thread:

```
class TestMultiPriority1 extends Thread{
public void run(){
System.out.println("running thread name is:"+Thread.currentThread().getName());
System.out.println("running thread priority is:"+Thread.currentThread().getPriority());
}
public static void main(String args[]){
TestMultiPriority1 m1=new TestMultiPriority1();
TestMultiPriority1 m2=new TestMultiPriority1();
m1.setPriority(Thread.MIN_PRIORITY);
m2.setPriority(Thread.MAX_PRIORITY);
m1.start();
m2.start();
}
}
```

Naming Thread and Current Thread

Naming Thread

The Thread class provides methods to change and get the name of a thread. By default, each thread has a name i.e. thread-0, thread-1 and so on. By we can change the name of the thread by using setName() method. The syntax of setName() and getName() methods are given below:

public String getName(): is used to return the name of a thread.

public void setName(String name): is used to change the name of a thread.

Example of naming a thread

```
class TestMultiNaming1 extends Thread{
public void run(){
System.out.println("running...");
}
public static void main(String args[]){
TestMultiNaming1 t1=new TestMultiNaming1();
TestMultiNaming1 t2=new TestMultiNaming1();
System.out.println("Name of t1:"+t1.getName());
System.out.println("Name of t2:"+t2.getName());
t1.start();
t2.start();
t1.setName("Sonoo Jaiswal");
System.out.println("After changing name of t1:"+t1.getName());
}
}
```

Current Thread

The currentThread() method returns a reference of currently executing thread.

public static Thread currentThread()

Example of currentThread() method

```
class TestMultiNaming2 extends Thread{
public void run(){
System.out.println(Thread.currentThread().getName());
}
public static void main(String args[]){
TestMultiNaming2 t1=new TestMultiNaming2();
TestMultiNaming2 t2=new TestMultiNaming2();
t1.start();
t2.start();
}
}
```

Synchronization in Java

Synchronization in java is the capability *to control the access of multiple threads to any shared resource.*

Java Synchronization is better option where we want to allow only one thread to access the shared resource.

Why use Synchronization?

The synchronization is mainly used to

- To prevent thread interference.
- To prevent consistency problem.

Types of Synchronization

There are two types of synchronization

- Process Synchronization
- Thread Synchronization

Here, we will discuss only thread synchronization.

Thread Synchronization

There are two types of thread synchronization mutual exclusive and inter-thread communication.

1. Mutual Exclusive

    a. Synchronized method.
    b. Synchronized block.
    c. static synchronization.

2. Cooperation (Inter-thread communication in java)

1. Mutual Exclusive

Mutual Exclusive helps keep threads from interfering with one another while sharing data. This can be done by three ways in java:

- by synchronized method
- by synchronized block
- by static synchronization

Concept of Lock in Java

Synchronization is built around an internal entity known as the lock or monitor. Every object has a lock associated with it. By convention, a thread that needs consistent access to an object's fields has to acquire the object's lock before accessing them, and then release the lock when it's done with them.

Understanding the problem without Synchronization

In this example, there is no synchronization, so output is inconsistent. Let's see the example:

```
class Table{
void printTable(int n){//method not synchronized
for(int i=1;i<=5;i++){
System.out.println(n*i);
try{
Thread.sleep(400);
}catch(Exception e){System.out.println(e);}
}
}
}
class MyThread1 extends Thread{
Table t;
MyThread1(Table t){
this.t=t;
}
public void run(){
t.printTable(5);
}
}
class MyThread2 extends Thread{
Table t;
MyThread2(Table t){
this.t=t;
}
public void run(){
t.printTable(100);
}
}
class TestSynchronization1{
public static void main(String args[]){
```

```
Table obj = new Table();//only one object
MyThread1 t1=new MyThread1(obj);
MyThread2 t2=new MyThread2(obj);
t1.start();
t2.start();
}
}
```

Java synchronized method

If you declare any method as synchronized, it is known as synchronized method.

Synchronized method is used to lock an object for any shared resource.

When a thread invokes a synchronized method, it automatically acquires the lock for that object and releases it when the thread completes its task.

```
//example of java synchronized method
class Table{
synchronized void printTable(int n){//synchronized method
for(int i=1;i<=5;i++){
System.out.println(n*i);
try{
Thread.sleep(400);
}catch(Exception e){System.out.println(e);}
}
}
}
class MyThread1 extends Thread{
Table t;
MyThread1(Table t){
this.t=t;
}
public void run(){
t.printTable(5);
}
}
class MyThread2 extends Thread{
Table t;
MyThread2(Table t){
this.t=t;
}
```

```
public void run(){
t.printTable(100);
}
}
public class TestSynchronization2{
public static void main(String args[]){
Table obj = new Table();//only one object
MyThread1 t1=new MyThread1(obj);
MyThread2 t2=new MyThread2(obj);
t1.start();
t2.start();
}
}
```

Inter-thread communication in Java

Inter-thread communication or Co-operation is all about allowing synchronized threads to communicate with each other.

Cooperation (Inter-thread communication) is a mechanism in which a thread is paused running in its critical section and another thread is allowed to enter (or lock) in the same critical section to be executed.It is implemented by following methods of Object class:

1. wait()
2. notify()
3. notifyAll()

1) wait() method

Causes current thread to release the lock and wait until either another thread invokes the notify() method or the notifyAll() method for this object, or a specified amount of time has elapsed.

The current thread must own this object's monitor, so it must be called from the synchronized method only otherwise it will throw exception.

public final void wait()throws InterruptedException - waits until object is notified.

public final void wait(long timeout)throws InterruptedException - waits for the specified amount of time.

2) notify() method

Wakes up a single thread that is waiting on this object's monitor. If any threads are waiting on this object, one of them is chosen to be awakened.

The choice is arbitrary and occurs at the discretion of the implementation. Syntax:

public final void notify()

3) notifyAll() method

Wakes up all threads that are waiting on this object's monitor. Syntax:

public final void notifyAll()

Understanding the process of inter-thread communication

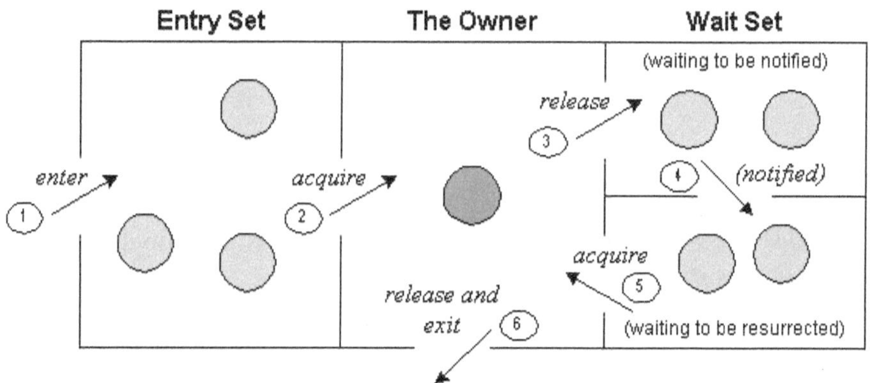

Interthread Communication

The point to point explanation of the above diagram is as follows:

Threads enter to acquire lock.

Lock is acquired by on thread.

Now thread goes to waiting state if you call wait() method on the object. Otherwise it releases the lock and exits.

If you call notify() or notifyAll() method, thread moves to the notified state (runnable state).

Now thread is available to acquire lock.

After completion of the task, thread releases the lock and exits the monitor state of the object.

Why wait(), notify() and notifyAll() methods are defined in Object class not Thread class?

It is because they are related to lock and object has a lock.

Difference between wait and sleep?

Let's see the important differences between wait and sleep methods.

wait()	sleep()
wait() method releases the lock	sleep() method doesn't release the lock.
is the method of Object class is the non-static method	is the method of Thread class is the static method
is the non-static method should be notified by notify() or notifyAll() methods	is the static method after the specified amount of time, sleep is completed.

Difference between sleep and wait method

Example of inter thread communication in java

```
class Customer{
int amount=10000;
synchronized void withdraw(int amount){
System.out.println("going to withdraw...");
if(this.amount<amount){
System.out.println("Less balance; waiting for deposit...");
try{wait();}catch(Exception e){}
}
this.amount-=amount;
System.out.println("withdraw completed...");
}
synchronized void deposit(int amount){
System.out.println("going to deposit...");
this.amount+=amount;
System.out.println("deposit completed... ");
notify();
}
}
```

```
class Test
{
public static void main(String args[]){
final Customer c=new Customer();
new Thread(){
public void run(){c.withdraw(15000);}
}.start();
new Thread(){
public void run(){c.deposit(10000);}
}.start();
}
}
```

More Practice Program:

1. Write a java program to blink image on the Frame continuously.

```
import java.awt.*;
import javax.swing.*;
class BlinkFrame extends JFrame implements Runnable
{
JLabel lbl;
boolean flag=false;
BlinkFrame()
{
setVisible(true);
setSize(500,500);
setLayout(new FlowLayout());
lbl=new JLabel(new ImageIcon(".\\workplace.jpg"));
add(lbl);
}
public void run()
{
while(true)
{
try
{
if(flag==true)
{
lbl.setVisible(true);
flag=false;
```

```
Thread.sleep(1000);
}
if(flag==false)
{
lbl.setVisible(false);
flag=true;
Thread.sleep(1000);
}
}
catch(Exception e){e.printStackTrace();}
}
}
}
class BlinkDemo
{
public static void main(String arg[])
{
BlinkFrame b= new BlinkFrame();
Thread t=new Thread(b);
t.start();
}
}
```

2. Write a program in java which will show lifecycle (creation, sleep, and dead) of a thread. Program should print randomly the name of thread and value of sleep time. The name of the thread should be hard coded through constructor. The sleep time of a thread will be a random integer in the range 0 to 4999.

```
class RandomThread1 extends Thread
{
int i=1;
RandomThread1(String name)
{
setName(name);
}
publicvoid run()
{
try
{
```

```
System.out.println(this.getName()+"\t Created");
while(i<=5)
{
int s=(int)(Math.random()*5000);
System.out.println("Thread\t"+this.getName()+"\tslcep                for\
t"+s+"Seconds");
i=i+1;
Thread.sleep(s);
}
System.out.println(""+this.getName()+"\tDead");
System.out.println(""+this.getName()+"\tDead");
}catch(Exception e){}
}
}
class RandomThread
{
publicstaticvoid main(String arg[]) throws Exception
{
RandomThread1 r1=new RandomThread1("Thrad1");
RandomThread1 r2=new RandomThread1("Thread2");
r1.start();
r2.start();
}
}
```

3. Write a java program to scroll the text from left to right and vice versa continuously

```
import java.awt.*;
publicclassTextMoveextends Frame implements Runnable {
int x, y, z;
Thread t;
TextMove() {
setVisible(true);
setSize(500,500);
x = 50;
y = 50;
z = 1;
t = new Thread(this);
t.start();
```

```
}
publicvoid mpostion() {
x = x + 10 * z;
if (x > this.getWidth())
z = -1;
if (x < 0)
z = 1;
}
publicvoid run() {
while (true) {
repaint();
mpostion();
try {
Thread.sleep(100);
} catch (Exception e) {
}
}
}
publicvoid paint(Graphics g) {
g.drawString("SSR College", x, y);
}
publicstaticvoid main(String arg[])
{
new TextMove();
}
}
```

4. Write a Multithreading program in java to display the number's between 1 to 100

continuously in a TextField by clicking on button. (use Runnable Interface).

```
import java.awt.*;
import javax.swing.*;
import java.awt.event.*;
class DisplayNumbersFrame extends JFrame implements Runnable,ActionListener
{
JButton btn;
JTextField t;
```

```
Thread th;
DisplayNumbersFrame()
{
setVisiblc(true);
setSize(500,500);
setLayout(new FlowLayout());
btn=new JButton("start");
t=new JTextField(20);
add(t);
add(btn);
btn.addActionListener(this);
}
public void actionPerformed(ActionEvent a)
{
th=new Thread(this);
th.start();
}
public void run()
{
try
{
while(true)
{
for(int i=1;i<=100;i++)
{
t.setText(""+i);
Thread.sleep(1000);
}
}
}
catch(Exception e){e.printStackTrace();}
}
}
class DisplayNumbers
{
public static void main(String arg[])
{
DisplayNumbersFrame b= new DisplayNumbersFrame();
```

```
}
}
```

CHAPTER III

Java Networking

Java Networking is a concept of connecting two or more computing devices together so that we can share resources.

Java socket programming provides facility to share data between different computing devices.

Advantage of Java Networking

- sharing resources
- centralize software management

Do You Know ?

- How to perform connection-oriented Socket Programming in networking?
- How to display the data of any online web page?
- How to get the IP address of any host name e.g. www.google.com?
- How to perform connection-less socket programming in networking?

Java Networking Terminology

The widely used java networking terminologies are given below:

1. IP Address
2. Protocol
3. Port Number
4. MAC Address
5. Connection-oriented and connection-less protocol
6. Socket

1) IP Address

IP address is a unique number assigned to a node of a network e.g. 192.168.0.1. It is composed of octets that range from 0 to 255.

It is a logical address that can be changed.

2) Protocol

A protocol is a set of rules basically that is followed for communication.

For example:

- TCP
- FTP
- Telnet
- SMTP
- POP etc.

3) Port Number

The port number is used to uniquely identify different applications. It acts as a communication endpoint between applications.

The port number is associated with the IP address for communication between two applications.

4) MAC Address

MAC (Media Access Control) Address is a unique identifier of NIC (Network Interface Controller). A network node can have multiple NIC but each with unique MAC.

5) Connection-oriented and connection-less protocol

In connection-oriented protocol, acknowledgement is sent by the receiver. So, it is reliable but slow. The example of connection-oriented protocol is TCP.

But, in connection-less protocol, acknowledgement is not sent by the receiver. So, it is not reliable but fast. The example of connection-less protocol is UDP.

6) Socket

A socket is an endpoint between two-way communication.

To perform socket programming java provides networking API, to use this API we need to import java.net package in the program.

Java InetAddress class

Java InetAddress class represents an IP address. The java.net.InetAddress class provides methods to get the IP of any host name *for example* www.javatpoint.com, www.google.com, www.facebook.com, etc.

An IP address is represented by 32-bit or 128-bit unsigned number. An instance of InetAddress represents the IP address with its corresponding host name. There are two types of address types: Unicast and Multicast. The Unicast is an identifier for a single interface whereas Multicast is an identifier for a set of interfaces.

Moreover, InetAddress has a cache mechanism to store successful and unsuccessful host name resolutions.

Commonly used methods of InetAddress class

- public static InetAddress getByName(String host) throws UnknownHostException- it returns the instance of InetAddress containing LocalHost IP and name.
- public static InetAddress getLocalHost() throws UnknownHostException- it returns the instance of InetAdddress containing local host name and address.
- public String getHostName()- it returns the host name of the IP address.
- public String getHostAddress()- it returns the IP address in string format.

Example of Java InetAddress class

Let's see a simple example of InetAddress class to get ip address of www.javatpoint.com website.

```
import java.io.*;
import java.net.*;
public class InetDemo{
public static void main(String[] args){
try{
InetAddress ip=InetAddress.getByName("www.javatpoint.com");
System.out.println("Host Name: "+ip.getHostName());
System.out.println("IP Address: "+ip.getHostAddress());
}catch(Exception e){System.out.println(e);}
}
}
```

The java.net package provides many classes to deal with networking applications in Java. A list of these classes is given below:

- DatagramPacket
- DatagramSocket
- InetAddress
- ServerSocket
- Socket

Java Socket Programming

Java Socket programming is used for communication between the applications running on different JRE.

Java Socket programming can be connection-oriented or connection-less.

Socket and ServerSocket classes are used for connection-oriented socket programming and DatagramSocket and DatagramPacket classes are used for connection-less socket programming.

The client in socket programming must know two information:

IP Address of Server, and

Port number.

Here, we are going to make one-way client and server communication. In this application, client sends a message to the server, server reads the message and prints it. Here, two classes are being used: Socket and ServerSocket. The Socket class is used to communicate client and server. Through this class, we can read and write message. The ServerSocket class is used at server-side. The accept() method of ServerSocket class blocks the console until the client is connected. After the successful connection of client, it returns the instance of Socket at server-side.

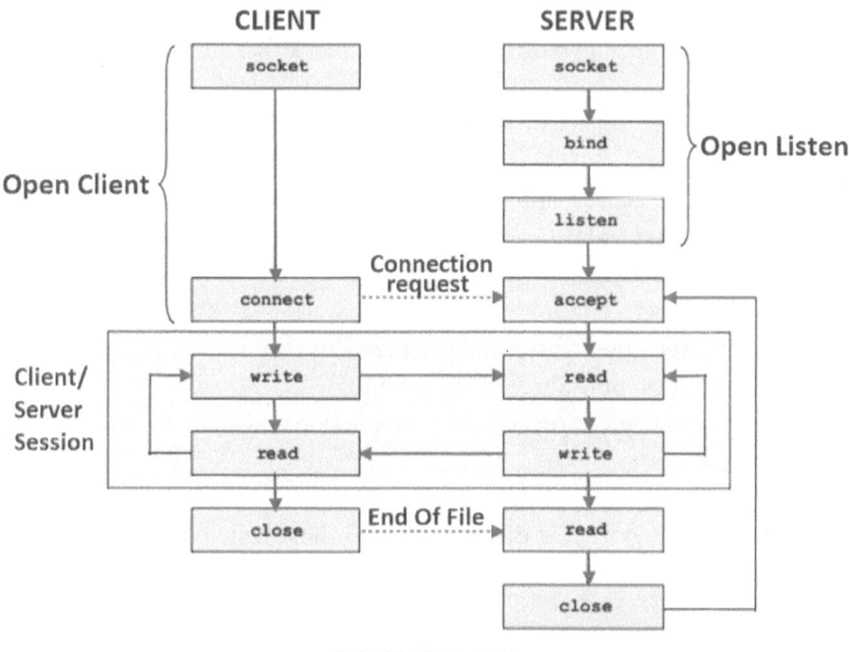

SOCKET API

Socket class

A socket is simply an endpoint for communications between the machines. The Socket class can be used to create a socket.

Important methods

- public InputStream getInputStream()- returns the InputStream attached with this socket.
- public OutputStream getOutputStream()- returns the OutputStream attached with this socket.
- public synchronized void close()- closes this socket.

ServerSocket class

The ServerSocket class can be used to create a server socket. This object is used to establish communication with the clients.

Important methods

- public Socket accept()- returns the socket and establish a connection between server and client.
- public synchronized void close()- closes the server socket.

Example of Java Socket Programming

Creating Server:

To create the server application, we need to create the instance of ServerSocket class. Here, we are using 6666 port number for the communication between the client and server. You may also choose any other port number. The accept() method waits for the client. If clients connects with the given port number, it returns an instance of Socket.

```
ServerSocket ss=new ServerSocket(6666);
Socket s=ss.accept();//establishes connection and waits for the client
```

Creating Client:

To create the client application, we need to create the instance of Socket class. Here, we need to pass the IP address or hostname of the Server and a port number. Here, we are using "localhost" because our server is running on same system.

```
Socket s=new Socket("localhost",6666);
```

Let's see a simple of Java socket programming where client sends a text and server receives and prints it.

File: MyServer.java

```
import java.io.*;
import java.net.*;
public class MyServer {
public static void main(String[] args){
try{
ServerSocket ss=new ServerSocket(3333);
Socket s=ss.accept();//establishes connection
DataInputStream dis=new DataInputStream(s.getInputStream());
String str=(String)dis.readUTF();
System.out.println("message= "+str);
ss.close();
}catch(Exception e){System.out.println(e);}
}
}
```

File: MyClient.java

```
import java.io.*;
import java.net.*;
public class MyClient {
public static void main(String[] args) {
try{
Socket s=new Socket("localhost",3333);
DataOutputStream dout=new DataOutputStream(s.getOutputStream());
dout.writeUTF("Hello Server");
dout.flush();
dout.close();
s.close();
}catch(Exception e){System.out.println(e);}
}
}
```

Example of Java Socket Programming (Read-Write both side)

In this example, client will write first to the server then server will receive and print the text. Then server will write to the client and client will receive and print the text. The step goes on.

File: MyServer1.java

```
import java.net.*;
```

```
import java.io.*;
class MyServer1{
public static void main(String args[])throws Exception{
ServerSocket ss=new ServerSocket(3333);
Socket s=ss.accept();
DataInputStream din=new DataInputStream(s.getInputStream());
DataOutputStream dout=new DataOutputStream(s.getOutputStream());
BufferedReader br=new BufferedReader(new
InputStreamReader(System.in));
String str="",str2="";
while(!str.equals("stop")){
str=din.readUTF();
System.out.println("client says: "+str);
str2=br.readLine();
dout.writeUTF(str2);
dout.flush();
}
din.close();
s.close();
ss.close();
}}
```

File: MyClient1.java

```
import java.net.*;
import java.io.*;
class MyClient1{
public static void main(String args[])throws Exception{
Socket s=new Socket("localhost",3333);
DataInputStream din=new DataInputStream(s.getInputStream());
DataOutputStream dout=new DataOutputStream(s.getOutputStream());
BufferedReader br=new BufferedReader(new
InputStreamReader(System.in));
String str="",str2="";
while(!str.equals("stop")){
str=br.readLine();
dout.writeUTF(str);
dout.flush();
str2=din.readUTF();
System.out.println("Server says: "+str2);
```

```
}
dout.close();
s.close();
}
}
```

Java DatagramSocket and DatagramPacket

Java DatagramSocket and DatagramPacket classes are used for connection-less socket programming.

Java DatagramSocket class

Java DatagramSocket class represents a connection-less socket for sending and receiving datagram packets.

A datagram is basically an information but there is no guarantee of its content, arrival or arrival time.

Commonly used Constructors of DatagramSocket class

DatagramSocket() throws SocketException: it creates a datagram socket and binds it with the available Port Number on the localhost machine.

DatagramSocket(int port) throws SocketException: it creates a datagram socket and binds it with the given Port Number.

DatagramSocket(int port, InetAddress address) throws SocketException: it creates a datagram socket and binds it with the specified port number and host address.

Java DatagramPacket class

Java DatagramPacket is a message that can be sent or received. If you send multiple packet, it may arrive in any order. Additionally, packet delivery is not guaranteed.

Commonly used Constructors of DatagramPacket class

DatagramPacket(byte[] barr, int length): it creates a datagram packet. This constructor is used to receive the packets.

DatagramPacket(byte[] barr, int length, InetAddress address, int port): it creates a datagram packet. This constructor is used to send the packets.

Example of Sending DatagramPacket by DatagramSocket

```
//DSender.java
import java.net.*;
public class DSender{
public static void main(String[] args) throws Exception {
DatagramSocket ds = new DatagramSocket();
```

```
String str = "Welcome java";
InetAddress ip = InetAddress.getByName("127.0.0.1");
DatagramPacket dp = new DatagramPacket(str.getBytes(), str.length(),
ip, 3000);
ds.send(dp);
ds.close();
}
}
```

Example of Receiving DatagramPacket by DatagramSocket

```
//DReceiver.java
import java.net.*;
public class DReceiver{
public static void main(String[] args) throws Exception {
DatagramSocket ds = new DatagramSocket(3000);
byte[] buf = new byte[1024];
DatagramPacket dp = new DatagramPacket(buf, 1024);
ds.receive(dp);
String str = new String(dp.getData(), 0, dp.getLength());
System.out.println(str);
ds.close();
}
}
```

CHAPTER IV

Servlet

Servlet technology is used to create a web application (resides at server side and generates a dynamic web page).

Servlet technology is robust and scalable because of java language. Before Servlet, CGI (Common Gateway Interface) scripting language was common as a server-side programming language. However, there were many disadvantages to this technology. We have discussed these disadvantages below.

There are many interfaces and classes in the Servlet API such as Servlet, GenericServlet, HttpServlet, ServletRequest, ServletResponse, etc.

What is a Servlet?

Servlet can be described in many ways, depending on the context.

Servlet is a technology which is used to create a web application.

Servlet is an API that provides many interfaces and classes including documentation.

Servlet is an interface that must be implemented for creating any Servlet.

Servlet is a class that extends the capabilities of the servers and responds to the incoming requests. It can respond to any requests.

Servlet is a web component that is deployed on the server to create a dynamic web page.

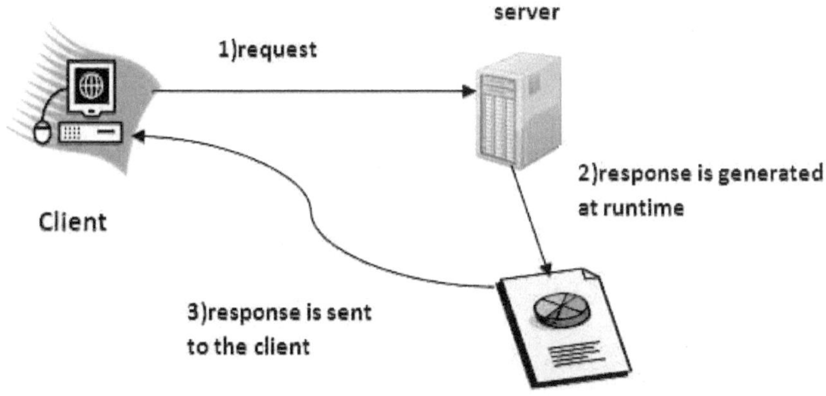

Servlet API
Interfaces in javax.servlet package
Classes in javax.servlet package
Interfaces in javax.servlet.http package
Classes in javax.servlet.http package

The javax.servlet and javax.servlet.http packages represent interfaces and classes for servlet api.

The javax.servlet package contains many interfaces and classes that are used by the servlet or web container. These are not specific to any protocol.

The javax.servlet.http package contains interfaces and classes that are responsible for http requests only.

Let's see what are the interfaces of javax.servlet package.

Interfaces in javax.servlet package

There are many interfaces in javax.servlet package. They are as follows:

- Servlet
- ServletRequest
- ServletResponse
- RequestDispatcher
- ServletConfig
- ServletContext
- SingleThreadModel
- Filter
- FilterConfig
- FilterChain
- ServletRequestListener
- ServletRequestAttributeListener
- ServletContextListener
- ServletContextAttributeListener

Classes in javax.servlet package

There are many classes in javax.servlet package. They are as follows:

- GenericServlet
- ServletInputStream
- ServletOutputStream
- ServletRequestWrapper

- ServletResponseWrapper
- ServletRequestEvent
- ServletContextEvent
- ServletRequestAttributeEvent
- ServletContextAttributeEvent
- ServletException

Life Cycle of a Servlet (Servlet Life Cycle)

1. Servlet class is loaded
2. Servlet instance is created
3. init method is invoked
4. service method is invoked
5. destroy method is invoked

The web container maintains the life cycle of a servlet instance. Let's see the life cycle of the servlet:

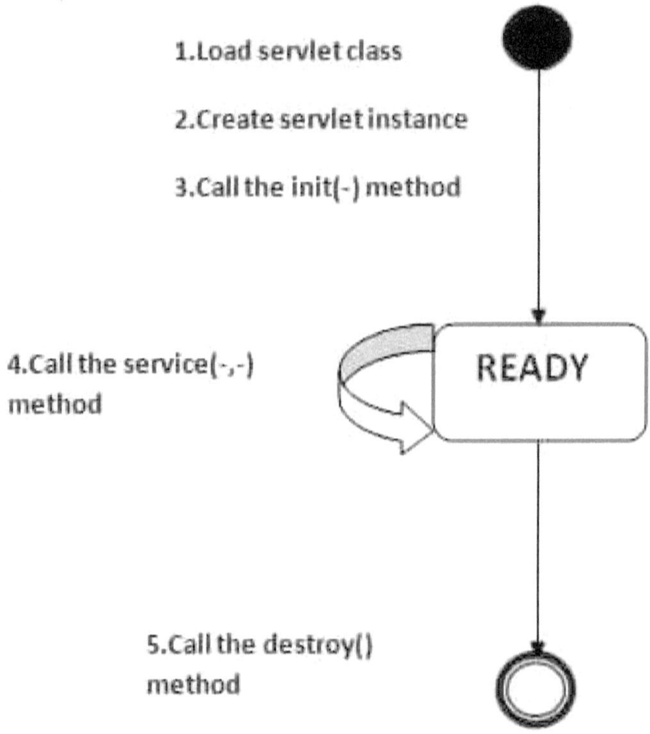

Life Cycle of Servlet

As displayed in the above diagram, there are three states of a servlet: new, ready and end. The servlet is in new state if servlet instance is created. After invoking the init() method, Servlet comes in the ready state. In the ready state, servlet performs all the tasks. When the web container invokes the destroy() method, it shifts to the end state.

1) Servlet class is loaded

The class loader is responsible to load the servlet class. The servlet class is loaded when the first request for the servlet is received by the web container.

2) Servlet instance is created

The web container creates the instance of a servlet after loading the servlet class. The servlet instance is created only once in the servlet life cycle.

3) init method is invoked

The web container calls the init method only once after creating the servlet instance. The init method is used to initialize the servlet. It is the life cycle method of the javax.servlet.Servlet interface. Syntax of the init method is given below:

public void init(ServletConfig config) throws ServletException

4) service method is invoked

The web container calls the service method each time when request for the servlet is received. If servlet is not initialized, it follows the first three steps as described above then calls the service method. If servlet is initialized, it calls the service method. Notice that servlet is initialized only once. The syntax of the service method of the Servlet interface is given below:

public void service(ServletRequest request, ServletResponse response)
throws ServletException, IOException

5) destroy method is invoked

The web container calls the destroy method before removing the servlet instance from the service. It gives the servlet an opportunity to clean up any resource for example memory, thread etc. The syntax of the destroy method of the Servlet interface is given below:

public void destroy()

Configuring Servlets and JSPs in Eclipse is a common task for Java web development. Below are the steps to set up a project in Eclipse for Servlet and JSP development:

Prerequisites

- Install Eclipse IDE for Java EE Developers.
- Install and configure a Java Development Kit (JDK).
- Download and configure an Apache Tomcat server.

Steps to Configure Servlet and JSP with Eclipse

Step 1: Install Eclipse IDE

Download and install the Eclipse IDE for Enterprise Java Developers from the official website.

Step 2: Install and Configure Tomcat Server

- Download the Apache Tomcat server from the Apache Tomcat website.
- Extract the downloaded Tomcat package.

- Configure Tomcat in Eclipse:

- Open Eclipse.
- Go to Window → Preferences → Server → Runtime Environments.
- Click Add.
- Select your Tomcat version (e.g., Apache Tomcat v10.0) and click Next.
- Browse to the Tomcat installation directory and finish the configuration.

Step 3: Create a Dynamic Web Project

- Go to File → New → Dynamic Web Project.
- Provide a project name (e.g., MyWebApp).
- Select a target runtime (choose Apache Tomcat from the dropdown).
- Set the Dynamic web module version (e.g., 4.0 for Servlet 4.0).
- Click Finish.

Example of Servlet:-

```
import java.io.*;
import javax.servlet.*;
import javax.servlet.http.*;
public class WelcomeServlet extends HttpServlet {
public void service(HttpServletRequest request, HttpServletResponse
response)
throws ServletException, IOException {
response.setContentType("text/html");
PrintWriter out = response.getWriter();
out.print("Welcome ");
}
}
```

doGet() and doPost() methods:-

protected void doGet(HttpServletRequest req, HttpServletResponse res) handles the GET request. It is invoked by the web container.

protected void doPost(HttpServletRequest req, HttpServletResponse res) handles the POST request. It is invoked by the web container.

doGet()

In doGet Method the parameters are appended to the URL and sent along with the information. Maximum size of data that can be sent using do Get it 240 bytes. Parameters are not encrypted. doGet method generally is used to query or to get some information from the server.

doGet is faster if we set the response content length since the same connection is used. Thus, increasing the performance. doGet should be important. doGet should be able to be repeated safely many times. doGet should be safe without any side effects for which user is held responsible.

doPost()

In doPost, parameters are sent in separate line in the body. There is no maximum size for data. Parameters are encrypted. doPost is generally used to update or posts some information to the server. do Post is slower compared to doGet since do Post does not write the content length.

This method does not need to be important Operations requested through POST can have side effects for which the user can be held accountable, for example, updating stored data or buying items online.

Difference Between doPost and doGet in Servlet

Http protocol mostly use either get or post methods to transfer the request. post method is generally used whenever you want to transfer secure data like password, bank account etc.

Get method	Post method
Get Request sends the request parameter as query string appended at the end of the request.	Post request send the request parameters as part of the http request body.
Get method is visible to every one (It will be displayed in the address bar of browser).	Post method variables are not displayed in the URL.
Restriction on form data, only ASCII characters allowed. Get methods have maximum size is 2000 character.	No Restriction on form data, Binary data is also allowed. Post methods have maximum size is 8 mb.
Restriction on form length, So URL length is restricted Remain in browser history.	No restriction on form data. Never remain the browser history.

Example of doGet()

```
import java.io. *;
import javax.servlet.*;
import javax.servlet.http.*;
publicclass WelcomeServlet extends HttpServlet {
publicvoid doGet(HttpServletRequest request, HttpServletResponse response)
throws ServletException, IOException {
response.setContentType("text/html");
PrintWriter out = response.getWriter();
String n=request.getParameter("userName");
out.print("Welcome "+n);
```

```
}
}
```

Servlet with JDBC:

Servlets are Java programs that run on a web server and handle HTTP requests and responses. Integrating

JDBC (Java Database Connectivity) allows servlets to interact with relational databases.

Key Points:

1. JDBC in Servlets:

o JDBC provides a standard API to connect and execute SQL queries on a database.

o Servlets use JDBC to fetch, insert, update, or delete data in the database.

2. Basic Workflow:

o Database Connection: Establish a connection using DriverManager.getConnection().

o SQL Execution: Use PreparedStatement or Statement to execute queries.

o Result Handling: Process the ResultSet for query results.

```
//Write a SERVLET program to display the details of Student (rno, Name,Per) on the browser
in tabular format. (Use database)
import javax.servlet.*;
import javax.servlet.annotation.WebServlet;
import javax.servlet.http.*;
import java.io.*;
import java.sql.*;
@WebServlet("/ServletJDBC1 ")
public class ServletJDBC1 extends HttpServlet {
public void service(HttpServletRequest request, HttpServletResponse response) throws IOException,
ServletException
{
PrintWriter out = response.getWriter();
try
{
Class.forName("oracle.jdbc.driver.OracleDriver");
```

```
Connection                                                    con
=DriverManager.getConnection("jdbc:oracle:thin:@localhost:1521:xe",
"system","root");
Statement st = con.createStatement();
ResultSet rs = st.executeQuery("Select * from student");
out.print("<table border=1>");
while(rs.next()){
out.print("<tr>");
out.print("<td>");
out.print(rs.getInt(1));
out.print("</td>");
out.print("<td>");
out.print(rs.getString(2));
out.print("</td>");
out.print("<td>");
out.print(rs.getInt(3));
out.print("</td>");
out.print("</tr>");
}
out.print("</table>");
}
catch(Exception e){
out.print(e);
}
}
}
```

// Write a SERVLET application to accept username and password, search them into database,

if found then

display appropriate message on the browser otherwise display error message.

```
import javax.servlet.*;
import javax.servlet.http.*;
import java.io.*;
import java.sql.*;
public class LoginCheck extends HttpServlet {
public void service(HttpServletRequest request, HttpServletResponse
response) throws IOException,
```

```
ServletException
{
PrintWriter out = response.getWriter();
try
{
Class.forName("oracle.jdbc.driver.OracleDriver");
Connection
con=DriverManager.getConnection("jdbc:oracle:thin:@localhost:1521:xe",
"system","root");
Statement st = con.createStatement();
String u=request.getParameter("t1");
String p=request.getParameter("pwd");
ResultSet rs = st.executeQuery("Select * from login where
uname='"+u+"' and password='"+p+"'");
if(rs.next())
out.print("Login Success");
else
out.print("Login UnSuccess");
}catch(Exception e){
out.print(e);
}
}
}
```

Session Tracking in Servlets

Session :

Session simply means a particular interval of time.

Session Tracking is a way to maintain state (data) of a user. It is also known as session management in servlet.

Http protocol is a stateless so we need to maintain state using session tracking techniques. Each time user requests to the server, server treats the request as the new request. So we need to maintain the state of an user to recognize to particular user.

HTTP is stateless that means each request is considered as the new request. It is shown in the figure given below:

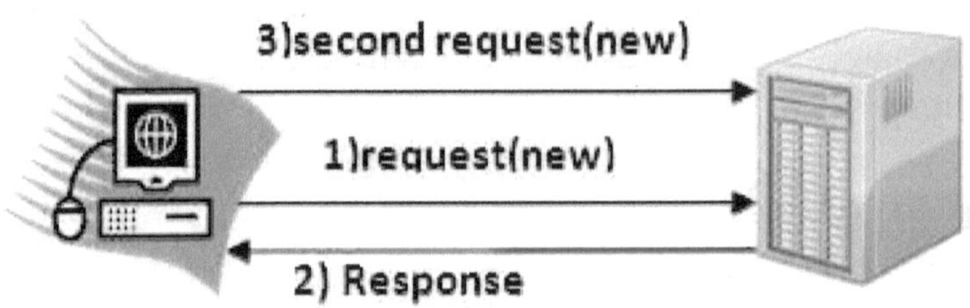

Why use Session Tracking?

It is used to recognize the particular user.

Session Tracking Techniques

There are four techniques used in Session tracking:

1. Hidden Form Field
2. URL Rewriting
3. HttpSession
4. Cookies

1. Hidden Form Field

Example of Hidden Form Field

In case of Hidden Form Field, a hidden (invisible) textfield is used for maintaining the state of a user.

In such case, we store the information in the hidden field and get it from another servlet. This approach is better if we have to submit form in all the pages and we don't want to depend on the browser.

Let's see the code to store value in hidden field.

<input type="hidden" name="uname" value="Vimal Jaiswal">

Here, uname is the hidden field name and Vimal Jaiswal is the hidden field value.

Real application of hidden form field

It is widely used in comment form of a website. In such case, we store page id or page name in the hidden field so that each page can be uniquely identified.

Advantage of Hidden Form Field

- It will always work whether cookie is disabled or not.

Disadvantage of Hidden Form Field:

- It is maintained at server side.
- Extra form submission is required on each page.
- Only textual information can be used.

Example of using Hidden Form Field

In this example, we are storing the name of the user in a hidden textfield and getting that value from another servlet.

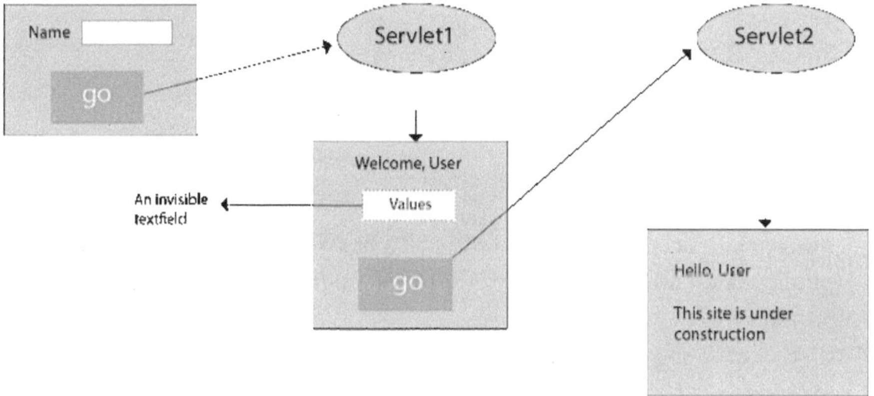

Example of Hidden Form Field

```
index.html
<form action="servlet1">
Name:<input type="text" name="userName"/><br/>
<input type="submit" value="go"/>
</form>
FirstServlet.java
import java.io.*;
```

```
import javax.servlet.*;
import javax.servlet.http.*;
public class FirstServlet extends HttpServlet {
public void doGet(HttpServletRequest request, HttpServletResponse response){
try{
response.setContentType("text/html");
PrintWriter out = response.getWriter();
String n=request.getParameter("userName");
out.print("Welcome "+n);
//creating form that have invisible textfield
out.print("<form action='servlet2'>");
out.print("<input type='hidden' name='uname' value='"+n+"'>");
out.print("<input type='submit' value='go'>");
out.print("</form>");
out.close();
}catch(Exception e){System.out.println(e);}
}
}
```

SecondServlet.java

```
import java.io.*;
import javax.servlet.*;
import javax.servlet.http.*;
public class SecondServlet extends HttpServlet {
public void doGet(HttpServletRequest request, HttpServletResponse response)
try{
response.setContentType("text/html");
PrintWriter out = response.getWriter();
//Getting the value from the hidden field
String n=request.getParameter("uname");
out.print("Hello "+n);
out.close();
}catch(Exception e){System.out.println(e);}
}
}
```

2.URL Rewriting

In URL rewriting, we append a token or identifier to the URL of the next Servlet or the next resource. We can send parameter name/value pairs using the following format:

url?name1=value1&name2=value2&??

A name and a value is separated using an equal = sign, a parameter name and value pair is separated from another parameter using the ampersand(&). When the user clicks the hyperlink, the parameter name and value pairs will be passed to the server. From a Servlet, we can use getParameter() method to obtain a parameter value.

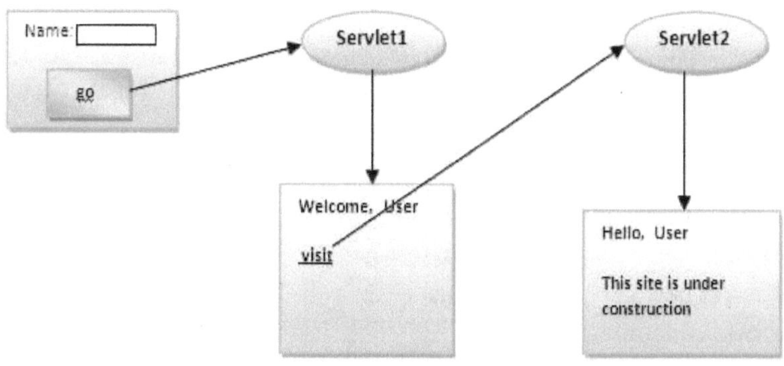

Example of URL Rewriting

Advantage of URL Rewriting

- It will always work whether cookie is disabled or not (browser independent).
- Extra form submission is not required on each page.

Disadvantage of URL Rewriting

- It will work only with links.
- It can send Only textual information.

Example of using URL Rewriting

In this example, we are maintaning the state of the user using link. For this purpose, we are appending the name of the user in the query string and getting the value from the query string in another page.

index.html

```
<form action="servlet1">
Name:<input type="text" name="userName"/><br/>
<input type="submit" value="go"/>
</form>
```

FirstServlet.java

```
import java.io.*;
import javax.servlet.*;
import javax.servlet.http.*;
public class FirstServlet extends HttpServlet {
public void doGet(HttpServletRequest request, HttpServletResponse response){
try{
response.setContentType("text/html");
PrintWriter out = response.getWriter();
String n=request.getParameter("userName");
out.print("Welcome "+n);
//appending the username in the query string
out.print("<a href=’servlet2?uname="+n+"‘>visit</a>");
out.close();
}catch(Exception e){System.out.println(e);}
}
}
```

SecondServlet.java

```
import java.io.*;
import javax.servlet.*;
import javax.servlet.http.*;
public class SecondServlet extends HttpServlet {
public void doGet(HttpServletRequest request, HttpServletResponse response)
try{
response.setContentType("text/html");
PrintWriter out = response.getWriter();
//getting value from the query string
String n=request.getParameter("uname");
```

```
out.print("Hello "+n);
out.close();
}catch(Exception e){System.out.println(e);}
}
}
```

3. HttpSession interface

In such case, container creates a session id for each user. The container uses this id to identify the particular user. An object of HttpSession can be used to perform two tasks:

1. bind objects
2. view and manipulate information about a session, such as the session identifier, creation time, and last accessed time.

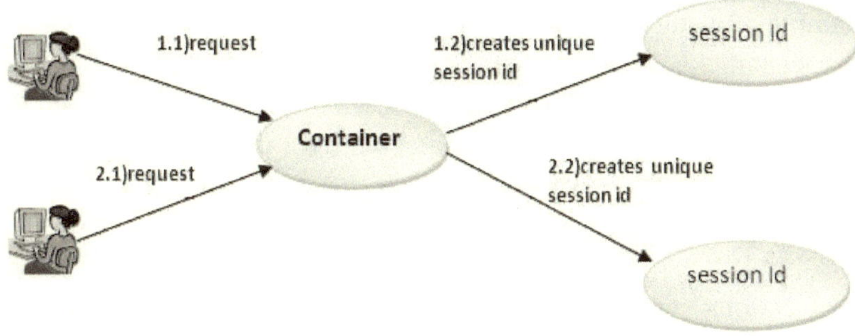

HTTP Session

How to get the HttpSession object ?

The HttpServletRequest interface provides two methods to get the object of HttpSession:

1. public HttpSession getSession():Returns the current session associated with this request, or if the request does not have a session, creates one.
2. public HttpSession getSession(boolean create):Returns the current HttpSession associated with this request or, if there is no current session and create is true, returns a new session.

Commonly used methods of HttpSession interface

1. public String getId():Returns a string containing the unique identifier value.
2. public long getCreationTime():Returns the time when this session was created, measured in milliseconds since midnight January 1, 1970 GMT.
3. public long getLastAccessedTime():Returns the last time the client sent a request associated with this session, as the number of milliseconds since midnight January 1, 1970 GMT.
4. public void invalidate ():Invalidates this session then unbinds any objects bound to it.
5. public void setAttribute(String name,Object object):sets the given object in the session scope.
6. public Object getAttribute(String name):Returns the attribute for the specified name.

Example of using HttpSession

In this example, we are setting the attribute in the session scope in one servlet and getting that value from the session scope in another servlet. To set the attribute in the session scope, we have used the setAttribute() method of HttpSession interface and to get the attribute, we have used the getAttribute method.

index.html

```
<form action="servlet1">
Name:<input type="text" name="userName"/><br/>
<input type="submit" value="go"/>
</form>
```

FirstServlet.java

```
import java.io.*;
import javax.servlet.*;
import javax.servlet.http.*;
public class FirstServlet extends HttpServlet {
public void doGet(HttpServletRequest request, HttpServletResponse response){
try{
response.setContentType("text/html");
PrintWriter out = response.getWriter();
String n=request.getParameter("userName");
```

```
out.print("Welcome "+n);
HttpSession session=request.getSession();
session.setAttribute("uname",n);
out.print("<a href='servlet2'>visit</a>");
out.close();
}catch(Exception e){System.out.println(e);}
}
}
//SecondServlet.java
import java.io.*;
import javax.servlet.*;
import javax.servlet.http.*;
public class SecondServlet extends HttpServlet {
public void doGet(HttpServletRequest request, HttpServletResponse response)
try{
response.setContentType("text/html");
PrintWriter out = response.getWriter();
HttpSession session=request.getSession(false);
String n=(String)session.getAttribute("uname");
out.print("Hello "+n);
out.close();
}catch(Exception e){System.out.println(e);}
}
}
```

Example2:-

This example illustrates about counting how many times the servlet is accessed. When first time servlet (CounterServlet) runs then session is created and value of the counter will be zero and after again accessing of servlet the counter value will be increased by one. In this program isNew() method is used whether session is new or old and getValue() method is used to get the value of counter.

Here is the source code of CounterServlet.java:

```
import java.io.*;
import javax.servlet.*;
import javax.servlet.http.*;
public class CounterServlet extends HttpServlet
{
```

```
public void service(HttpServletRequest request, HttpServletResponse response)
{
HttpScssion session = request.getSession(true);
PrintWriter pw = response.getWriter();
Integer count = new Integer(0);
if (session.isNew())
{
count=0;
}
else
{
Integer oldcount =(Integer)session.getValue("count");
if (oldcount != null) {
count = new Integer(oldcount.intValue() + 1);
}
}
session.putValue("count", count);
out.println("No. of times page visited="+count);
}
}
```

4. Cookies in Servlet

A cookie is a small piece of information that is persisted between the multiple client requests.

A cookie has a name, a single value, and optional attributes such as a comment, path and domain qualifiers, a maximum age, and a version number.

How Cookie works

By default, each request is considered as a new request. In cookies technique, we add cookie with response from the servlet. So cookie is stored in the cache of the browser. After that if request is sent by the user, cookie is added with request by default. Thus, we recognize the user as the old user.

Types of Cookie

There are 2 types of cookies in servlets.

1. Non-persistent cookie
2. Persistent cookie

1. Non-persistent cookie

It is valid for single session only. It is removed each time when user closes the browser.

2. Persistent cookie

It is valid for multiple session. It is not removed each time when user closes the browser. It is removed only if user logout or sign-out.

Advantage of Cookies

- Simplest technique of maintaining the state.
- Cookies are maintained at client side.

Disadvantage of Cookies

- It will not work if cookie is disabled from the browser.
- Only textual information can be set in Cookie object.

Cookie class

Cookie() constructs a cookie.

Cookie(String name, String value) constructs a cookie with a specified name and value.

javax.servlet.http.Cookie class provides the functionality of using cookies. It provides a lot of useful methods for cookies.

Constructor of Cookie class

Useful Methods of Cookie class

There are given some commonly used methods of the Cookie class.

- public void setMaxAge(int expiry) -Sets the maximum age of the cookie in seconds.
- public String getName() -Returns the name of the cookie. The name cannot be changed after creation.
- public String getValue() - Returns the value of the cookie.
- public void setName(String name)- changes the name of the cookie.
- public void setValue(String value)- changes the value of the cookie.

Other methods required for using Cookies

For adding cookie or getting the value from the cookie, we need some methods provided by other interfaces.

They are:

public void addCookie(Cookie ck): method of HttpServletResponse interface is usedto add cookie in response object.

public Cookie[] getCookies(): method of HttpServletRequest interface is used to return all the cookies from the browser.

How to create Cookie?

Let's see the simple code to create cookie.

```
Cookie ck=new Cookie("user","sonoo jaiswal");//creating cookie object
response.addCookie(ck);//adding cookie in the response
```

How to delete Cookie?

Let's see the simple code to delete cookie. It is mainly used to logout or signout the user.

```
Cookie ck=new Cookie("user","“) ;//deleting value of cookie
ck.setMaxAge(0);//changing the maximum age to 0 seconds
response.addCookie(ck);//adding cookie in the response
```

How to get Cookies?

Let's see the simple code to get all the cookies.

```
Cookie ck[]=request.getCookies();
for(int i=0;i<ck.length;i++)
{
out.print("<br>"+ck[i].getName()+"        "+ck[i].getValue());//printing name and value of cookie
}
```

Simple example of Servlet Cookies

In this example, we are storing the name of the user in the cookie object and accessing it in another servlet. As we know well that session corresponds to the particular user. So if you access it from too many browsers with different values, you will get the different value.

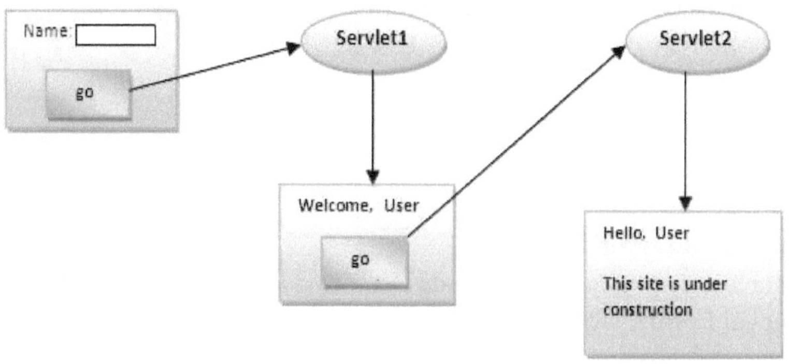

Example of Cokkie

index.html

```
<form action="servlet1" method="post">
Name:<input type="text" name="userName"/><br/>
<input type="submit" value="go"/>
</form>
```

FirstServlet.java

```
import java.io.*;
import javax.servlet.*;
import javax.servlet.http.*;
publicclass FirstServlet extends HttpServlet {
publicvoid doPost(HttpServletRequest request, HttpServletResponse response){
try{
response.setContentType("text/html");
PrintWriter out = response.getWriter();
String n=request.getParameter("userName");
out.print("Welcome "+n);
Cookie ck=new Cookie("uname",n);//creating cookie object
response.addCookie(ck);//adding cookie in the response
//creating submit button
out.print("<form action='servlet2'>");
out.print("<input type='submit' value='go'>");
```

```
out.print("</form>");
out.close();
}catch(Exception e){System.out.println(e);}
}
}
```

SecondServlet.java

```
import java.io.*;
import javax.servlet.*;
import javax.servlet.http.*;
publicclass SecondServlet extends HttpServlet {
publicvoid doPost(HttpServletRequest request, HttpServletResponse response){
try{
response.setContentType("text/html");
PrintWriter out = response.getWriter();
Cookie ck[]=request.getCookies();
out.print("Hello "+ck[0].getValue());
out.close();
}catch(Exception e){System.out.println(e);}
}
}
```

RequestDispatcher in Servlet

RequestDispatcher Interface

The RequestDispatcher interface provides the facility of dispatching the request to another resource it may be html, servlet or jsp. This interface can also be used to include the content of another resource also. It is one of the way of servlet collaboration.

There are two methods defined in the RequestDispatcher interface.

Methods of RequestDispatcher interface

The RequestDispatcher interface provides two methods. They are:

public void forward(ServletRequest request,ServletResponse response) throws ServletException,java.io.IOException:

Forwards a request from a servlet to another resource (servlet, JSP file, or HTML file) on the server.

public void include(ServletRequest request,ServletResponse response) throws ServletException,java.io.IOException:

Includes the content of a resource (servlet, JSP page, or HTML file) in the response.

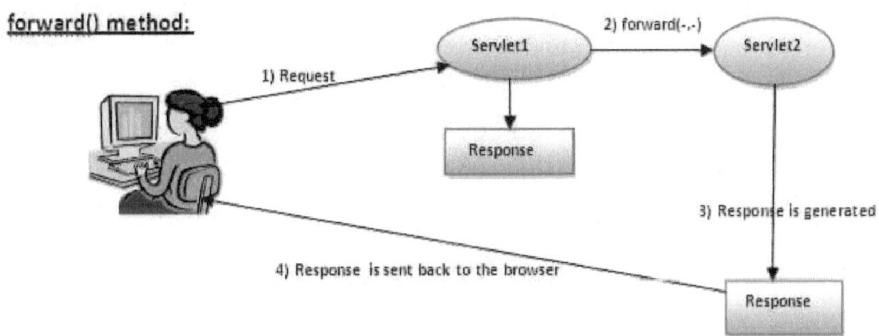

fig. forward() method

As you see in the above figure, response of second servlet is sent to the client. Response of the first servlet is not displayed to the user.

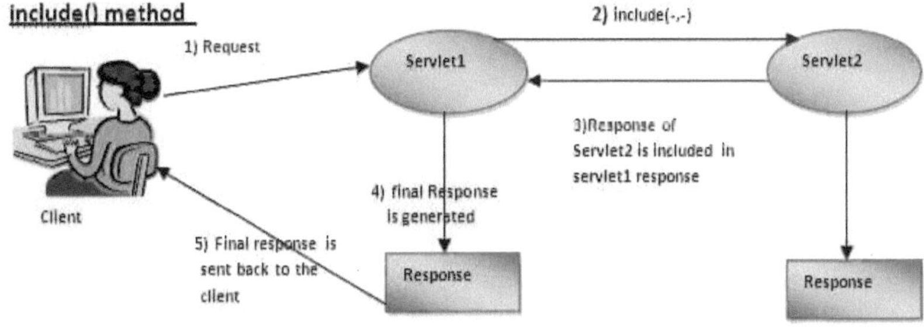

fig. include() method

As you see in the above figure, response of second servlet is included in the Response of the first servlet .

How to get the object of RequestDispatcher

The getRequestDispatcher() method of ServletRequest interface returns the object of RequestDispatcher.

Syntax of getRequestDispatcher method

public RequestDispatcher getRequestDispatcher(String resource);

Example of using getRequestDispatcher method

RequestDispatcher rd=request.getRequestDispatcher("servlet2");

//servlet2 is the url-pattern of the second servlet

rd.forward(request, response);//method may be include or forward

Example of RequestDispatcher interface

In this example, we are validating the password entered by the user. If password is servlet, it will forward the request to the WelcomeServlet, otherwise will show an error message: sorry username or password error!. In this program, we are cheking for hardcoded information. But you can check it to the database also that we will see in the development chapter. In this example, we have created following files:

index.html file: for getting input from the user.

Login.java file: a servlet class for processing the response. If password is servlet, it will forward the request to the welcome servlet.

WelcomeServlet.java file: a servlet class for displaying the welcome message.

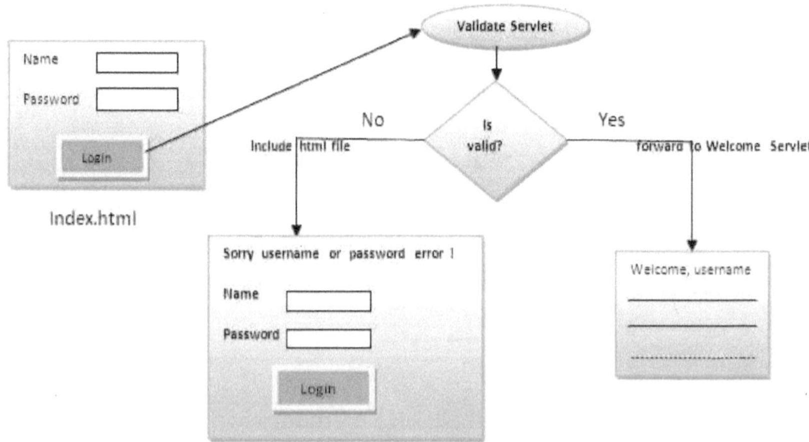

Example of RequestDispatcher

```
//index.html
<form action="servlet1" method="post">
Name:<input type="text" name="userName"/><br/>
Password:<input type="password" name="userPass"/><br/>
<input type="submit" value="login"/>
</form>
//Login.java
import java.io.*;
import javax.servlet.*;
import javax.servlet.http.*;
publicclass Login extends HttpServlet {
publicvoid doPost(HttpServletRequest request, HttpServletResponse
response)
throws ServletException, IOException {
response.setContentType("text/html");
PrintWriter out = response.getWriter();
String n=request.getParameter("userName");
String p=request.getParameter("userPass");
if(p.equals("servlet")){
RequestDispatcher
rd=request.getRequestDispatcher("WelcomeServlet");
rd.forward(request, response);
}
else{
out.print("Sorry UserName or Password Error!");
RequestDispatcher rd=request.getRequestDispatcher("/index.html");
rd.include(request, response);
}
}
}
//WelcomeServlet.java
import java.io.*;
import javax.servlet.*;
import javax.servlet.http.*;
publicclass WelcomeServlet extends HttpServlet {
```

publicvoid doPost(HttpServletRequest request, HttpServletResponse response)

throws ServletException, IOException {

response.setContentType("text/html");

PrintWriter out = response.getWriter();

String n=request.getParameter("userName");

out.print("Welcome "+n);

}

}

SendRedirect in servlet

The sendRedirect() method of HttpServletResponse interface can be used to redirect response

to another resource, it may be servlet, jsp or html file.

It accepts relative as well as absolute URL.

It works at client side because it uses the url bar of the browser to make another request.

So, it can work inside and outside the server.

Difference between forward() and sendRedirect() method

There are many differences between the forward() method of RequestDispatcher

and sendRedirect() method of HttpServletResponse interface.

They are given below:

forward() method

The forward() method works at server side.

- It sends the same request and response objects to another servlet.
- It can work within the server only.

Example:
request.getRequestDispacher("servlet2").forward(request,response);

sendRedirect() method

- The sendRedirect() method works at client side.
- It always sends a new request.
- It can be used within and outside the server.

Example: response.sendRedirect("servlet2");

Syntax of sendRedirect() method

```
public void sendRedirect(String URL)throws IOException;
```

Example of sendRedirect() method

```
response.sendRedirect("http://www.javatpoint.com");
```

Example of sendRedirect method in servlet

In this example, we are redirecting the request to the google server.

Notice that sendRedirect method works at client side, that is why we can our request to anywhere.

We can send our request within and outside the server.

```
//DemoServlet.java
import java.io.*;
import javax.scrvlct.*;
import javax.servlet.http.*;
public class DemoServlet extends HttpServlet{
public void doGet(HttpServletRequest req,HttpServletResponse res)
throws ServletException,IOException
{
res.setContentType("text/html");
PrintWriter pw=res.getWriter();
response.sendRedirect("http://www.google.com");
pw.close();
}
}
```

Example2: Creating custom google search using sendRedirect

In this example, we are using sendRedirect method to send request to google server with the

request data.

```
//index.html
<html>
<head>
<title>sendRedirect example</title>
</head>
<body>
<form action="MySearcher">
<input type="text" name="name">
<input type="submit" value="Google Search">
</form>
</body>
</html>
```

```
//MySearcher.java
import java.io.IOException;
import javax.servlet.ServletException;
import javax.servlet.http.HttpServlet;
import javax.servlet.http.HttpServletRequest;
import javax.servlet.http.HttpServletResponse;
public class MySearcher extends HttpServlet {
protected void doGet(HttpServletRequest request, HttpServletResponse
response)
throws ServletException, IOException {
String name=request.getParameter("name");
response.sendRedirect("https://www.google.co.in/#q="+name);
}
}
```

CHAPTER V

JSP (JAVA Server Pages)

JSP technology is used to create web application just like Servlet technology. It can be thought of as an extension to Servlet because it provides more functionality than servlet such as expression language, JSTL, etc.

A JSP page consists of HTML tags and JSP tags. The JSP pages are easier to maintain than Servlet because we can separate designing and development. It provides some additional features such as Expression Language, Custom Tags, etc.

Advantages of JSP over Servlet

There are many advantages of JSP over the Servlet. They are as follows:

1) Extension to Servlet

JSP technology is the extension to Servlet technology. We can use all the features of the Servlet in JSP. In addition to, we can use implicit objects, predefined tags, expression language and Custom tags in JSP, that makes JSP development easy.

2) Easy to maintain

JSP can be easily managed because we can easily separate our business logic with presentation logic. In Servlet technology, we mix our business logic with the presentation logic.

3) Fast Development: No need to recompile and redeploy

If JSP page is modified, we don't need to recompile and redeploy the project. The Servlet code needs to be updated and recompiled if we have to change the look and feel of the application.

4) Less code than Servlet

In JSP, we can use many tags such as action tags, JSTL, custom tags, etc. that reduces the code. Moreover, we can use EL, implicit objects, etc.

The Lifecycle of a JSP Page

The JSP pages follow these phases:

- Translation of JSP Page
- Compilation of JSP Page
- Classloading (the classloader loads class file)
- Instantiation (Object of the Generated Servlet is created).
- Initialization (the container invokes jspInit() method).

- Request processing (the container invokes _jspService() method).
- Destroy (the container invokes jspDestroy() method).

Note: jspInit(), _jspService() and jspDestroy() are the life cycle methods of JSP.

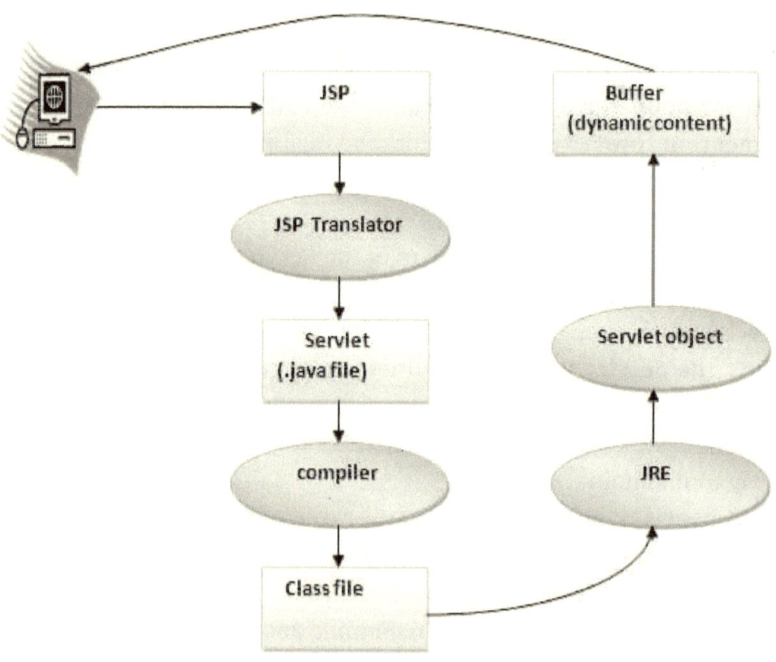

JSP page translation at server side

As depicted in the above diagram, JSP page is translated into Servlet by the help of JSP translator. The JSP translator is a part of the web server which is responsible for translating the JSP page into Servlet. After that, Servlet page is compiled by the compiler and gets converted into the class file. Moreover, all the processes that happen in Servlet are performed on JSP later like initialization, committing response to the browser and destroy.

Creating a simple JSP Page:

Creating a JSP (Java Server Pages) file in Eclipse is straightforward. Follow these steps:

Steps to Create a JSP Page in Eclipse

Step 1: Set Up Your Project

- Open Eclipse.
- Create a Dynamic Web Project:
- Go to File → New → Dynamic Web Project.
- Enter a name for the project (e.g., MyWebApp).
- Select your server runtime (e.g., Apache Tomcat) and click Finish.

Step 2: Create a JSP File

Locate the WebContent Folder:

In the Project Explorer, expand your project folder.

Locate the WebContent directory (this is where JSP files are typically placed).

Create the JSP File:

- Right-click on the WebContent folder → New → JSP File.
- In the dialog box, provide a name for your JSP file (e.g., index.jsp).
- Click Finish.

To create the first JSP page, write some HTML code as given below, and save it by .jsp extension. We have saved this file as index.jsp. Put it in a folder and paste the folder in the web-apps directory in apache tomcat to run the JSP page.

index.jsp

Let's see the simple example of JSP where we are using the scriptlet tag to put Java code in the JSP page. We will learn scriptlet tag later.

```
<html>
<body>
<% out.print(2*5); %>
</body>
</html>
```

JSP Scriptlet tag (Scripting elements)

- Scripting elements
- JSP scriptlet tag

Example of JSP scriptlet tag

Example of JSP scriptlet tag that prints the user name

In JSP, java code can be written inside the jsp page using the scriptlet tag. Let's see what are the scripting elements first.

JSP Scripting elements

The scripting elements provides the ability to insert java code inside the jsp.

There are three types of scripting elements:

1. scriptlet tag
2. expression tag
3. declaration tag

1. JSP scriptlet tag

A scriptlet tag is used to execute java source code in JSP. Syntax is as follows:

```
<% java source code %>
```

Example of JSP scriptlet tag

In this example, we are displaying a welcome message.

```
<html>
<body>
<% out.print("welcome to jsp"); %>
</body>
</html>
```

Example of JSP scriptlet tag that prints the user name

In this example, we have created two files index.html and welcome.jsp. The index.html file gets the username from the user and the welcome.jsp file prints the username with the welcome message.

File: index.html

```
<html>
<body>
<form action="welcome.jsp">
<input type="text" name="uname">
<input type="submit" value="go"><br/>
</form>
</body>
</html>
```

File: welcome.jsp

```
<html>
<body>
```

```
<%
String name=request.getParameter("uname");
out.print("welcome "+name);
%>
</form>
</body>
</html>
```

2. JSP expression tag

The code placed within **JSP expression tag** is *written to the output stream of the response*. So you need not write out.print() to write data. It is mainly used to print the values of variable or method.

Syntax of JSP expression tag

```
<%= statement %>
```

Example of JSP expression tag

In this example of jsp expression tag, we are simply displaying a welcome message.

```
<html>
<body>
<%= "welcome to jsp" %>
</body>
</html>
```

Example of JSP expression tag that prints current time

To display the current time, we have used the getTime() method of Calendar class. The getTime() is an instance method of Calendar class, so we have called it after getting the instance of Calendar class by the getInstance() method.

index.jsp

```
<html>
<body>
Current Time: <%= java.util.Calendar.getInstance().getTime() %>
</body>
</html>
```

Example of JSP expression tag that prints the user name

In this example, we are printing the username using the expression tag. The index.html file gets the username and sends the request to the welcome.jsp file, which displays the username.

File: index.jsp

```
<html>
```

```
<body>
<form action="welcome.jsp">
<input type="text" name="uname"><br/>
<input type="submit" value="go">
</form>
</body>
</html>
```

File: welcome.jsp

```
<html>
<body>
<%= "Welcome "+request.getParameter("uname") %>
</body>
</html>
```

3. JSP Declaration Tag

The **JSP declaration tag** is used *to declare fields and methods.*

The code written inside the jsp declaration tag is placed outside the service() method of auto generated servlet.

So, it doesn't get memory at each request.

Syntax of JSP declaration tag

The syntax of the declaration tag is as follows:

```
<%! field or method declaration %>
```

Difference between JSP Scriptlet tag and Declaration tag

JSP Scriptlet Tag	JSP Declaration Tag
The jsp scriptlet tag can only declare variables not methods.	The jsp declaration tag can declare variables as well as methods.
The declaration of scriptlet tag is placed inside the _jspService() method.	The declaration of jsp declaration tag is placed outside the _jspService() method.

Example of JSP declaration tag that declares field

In this example of JSP declaration tag, we are declaring the field and printing the value of the declared field using the jsp expression tag.

index.jsp

```
<html>
<body>
<%! int data=50; %>
<%= "Value of the variable is:"+data %>
</body>
</html>
```

Example of JSP declaration tag that declares method

In this example of JSP declaration tag, we are defining the method which returns the cube of given number and calling this method from the jsp expression tag. But we can also use jsp scriptlet tag to call the declared method.

index.jsp

```
<html>
<body>
<%!
int cube(int n){
return n*n*n*;
}
%>
<%= "Cube of 3 is:"+cube(3) %>
</body>
</html>
```

JSP directives

The jsp directives are messages that tells the web container how to translate a JSP page

into the corresponding servlet.

There are three types of directives:

1. page directive
2. include directive
3. taglib directive

Syntax of JSP Directive

```
<%@ directive attribute="value" %>
```

1. JSP page directive

The page directive defines attributes that apply to an entire JSP page.

Syntax of JSP page directive

```
<%@ page attribute="value" %>
```

Attributes of JSP page directive

Import, contentType, extends, buffer, language, session, errorPage , isErrorPage

1)import

The import attribute is used to import class,interface or all the members of a package.It is similar to

import keyword in java class or interface.

Example of import attribute

```
<html>
<body>
<%@ page import="java.util.Date" %>
Today is: <%= new Date() %>
</body>
</html>
```

2)contentType

The contentType attribute defines the MIME(Multipurpose Internet Mail Extension) type of the

HTTP response.The default value is "text/html;charset=ISO-8859-1".

Example of contentType attribute

```
<html>
<body>
<%@ page contentType=application/msword %>
Today is: <%= new java.util.Date() %>
</body>
</html>
```

3)extends

The extends attribute defines the parent class that will be inherited by the generated servlet.

It is rarely used.

4)buffer

The buffer attribute sets the buffer size in kilobytes to handle output generated by the JSP page.

The default size of the buffer is 8Kb.

Example of buffer attribute

```
<html>
```

```
<body>
<%@ page buffer="16kb" %>
Today is: <%= new java.util.Date() %>
</body>
</html>
```

6)language

The language attribute specifies the scripting language used in the JSP page. The default value is "java".

7)errorPage

The errorPage attribute is used to define the error page, if exception occurs in the current page,

it will be redirected to the error page.

Example of errorPage attribute

```
//index.jsp
<html>
<body>
<%@ page errorPage="myerrorpage.jsp" %>
<%= 100/0 %>
</body>
</html>
```

8)isErrorPage

The isErrorPage attribute is used to declare that the current page is the error page.

Note: The exception object can only be used in the error page.

Example of isErrorPage attribute

```
//myerrorpage.jsp
<html>
<body>
<%@ page isErrorPage="true" %>
Sorry an exception occured!<br/>
The exception is: <%= exception %>
</body>
</html>
```

2. JSP Include Directive

The include directive is used to include the contents of any resource it may be jsp file, html file or

text file. The include directive includes the original content of the included resource at page translation time (the jsp page is translated only once so it will be better to include static resource).

Advantage of Include directive

Code Reusability

Syntax of include directive

```
<%@ include file="resourceName" %>
```

Example of include directive

In this example, we are including the content of the header.html file. To run this example you must create an header.html file.

```
<html>
<body>
<%@ include file="header.html" %>
Today is: <%= java.util.Calendar.getInstance().getTime() %>
</body>
</html>
```

3. JSP Taglib directive

The JSP taglib directive is used to define a tag library that defines many tags. We use the

TLD (Tag Library Descriptor) file to define the tags. In the custom tag section, we will use this tag so

it will be better to learn it in custom tag.

Syntax JSP Taglib directive

```
<%@ taglib uri="uriofthetaglibrary" prefix="prefixoftaglibrary" %>
```

Example of JSP Taglib directive

In this example, we are using our tag named currentDate. To use this tag, we must specify

the taglib directive so the container may get information about the tag.

```
<html>
<body>
<%@ taglib uri="http://www.javatpoint.com/tags" prefix="mytag" %>
<mytag:currentDate/>
</body>
</html>
```

JSP Implicit Objects

There are 9 jsp implicit objects. These objects are *created by the web container* that are available

to all the jsp pages.

The available implicit objects are out, request, config, session, application etc.

A list of the 9 implicit objects is given below:

Object Type

out JspWriter

request HttpServletRequest

response HttpServletResponse

config ServletConfig

application ServletContext

session HttpSession

pageContext PageContext

page Object

exception Throwable

1. JSP out implicit object

For writing any data to the buffer, JSP provides an implicit object named out.

It is the object of JspWriter. In case of servlet you need to write:

PrintWriter out=response.getWriter();

But in JSP, you don't need to write this code.

Example of out implicit object

In this example we are simply displaying date and time.

index.jsp

```
<html>
<body>
<% out.print("Today is:"+java.util.Calendar.getInstance().getTime());
%>
</body>
</html>
```

2. JSP request implicit object

The JSP request is an implicit object of type HttpServletRequest i.e. created for each jsp request

by the web container. It can be used to get request information such as parameter,

header information, remote address, server name, server port, content type, character encoding etc.

It can also be used to set, get and remove attributes from the jsp request scope.

Let's see the simple example of request implicit object where we are printing the name of the user with welcome message.

Example of JSP request implicit object

index.html

```
<form action="welcome.jsp">
<input type="text" name="uname">
<input type="submit" value="go"><br/>
</form>
```

welcome.jsp

```
<%
String name=request.getParameter("uname");
out.print("welcome "+name);
%>
```

3. JSP response implicit object

In JSP, response is an implicit object of type HttpServletResponse. The instance of HttpServletResponse

is created by the web container for each jsp request.

It can be used to add or manipulate response such as redirect response to another resource, send error etc.

Let's see the example of response implicit object where we are redirecting the response to the Google.

Example of response implicit object

index.html

```
<form action="welcome.jsp">
<input type="text" name="uname">
<input type="submit" value="go"><br/>
</form>
```

welcome.jsp

```
<%
response.sendRedirect("http://www.google.com");
%>
```

4. session implicit object

In JSP, session is an implicit object of type HttpSession.The Java developer can use this object

to set,get or remove attribute or to get session information.

Example of session implicit object

index.html

```
<html>
```

```
<body>
<form action="welcome.jsp">
<input type="text" name="uname">
<input type="submit" value="go"><br/>
</form>
</body>
</html>
welcome.jsp
<html>
<body>
<%
String name=request.getParameter("uname");
out.print("Welcome "+name);
session.setAttribute("user",name);
<a href="second.jsp">second jsp page</a>
%>
</body>
</html>
second.jsp
<html>
<body>
<%
String name=(String)session.getAttribute("user");
out.print("Hello "+name);
%>
</body>
</html>
```

5.exception implicit object

In JSP, exception is an implicit object of type java.lang.Throwable class. This object can be used to

print the exception. But it can only be used in error pages.It is better to learn it after page directive.

Let’s see a simple example:

Example of exception implicit object:

```
error.jsp
<%@ page isErrorPage="true" %>
<html>
<body>
```

```
Sorry following exception occured:<%= exception %>
</body> </html>
```

More practice example:-

Example1:- shows how you can use JSP page to count the total number of hits on a particular page.

If you want to count the total number of hits of your website then you will have to include the same

code in all the JSP pages.

```
<%@ page import = "java.io.*,java.util.*" %>
<html>
<head>
<title>Application object in JSP</title>
</head>
<body>
<%
Integer hitsCount = (Integer)application.getAttribute("hitCounter");
if( hitsCount ==null || hitsCount == 0 ) {
/* First visit */
out.println("Welcome to my website!");
hitsCount = 1;
} else {
/* return visit */
out.println("Welcome back to my website!");
hitsCount += 1;
}
application.setAttribute("hitCounter", hitsCount);
%>
<center>
<p>Total number of visits: <%= hitsCount%></p>
</center>
</body> </html>
```

Example 2:Write a JSP script to validate given E-Mail ID.

```
//mailinput.html
<!DOCTYPE html>
<html lang="en">
<head>
<meta charset="UTF-8">
<meta http-equiv="X-UA-Compatible" content="IE=edge">
```

```
<meta name="viewport" content="width=device-width, initial-scale=1.0">
<title>Email Verification</title>
</head>
<body>
<form action="emailvalid.jsp">
Enter Email : <input type="text" name="email">
<input type="submit">
</form>
</body>
</html>
//emailvalid.jsp
<%
String e = request.getParameter("email");
String exp = "^[A-Za-z0-9+_.-]+@(.+)$";
if(e.matches(exp)){
out.print("Valid Email");
}
else{
out.print("Invalid Email");
}
%>
```

JSP with JDBC:

JSP pages that run on a web server and handle HTTP requests and responses. Integrating

JDBC (Java Database Connectivity) allows JSP to interact with relational databases.

Key Points:

1. JDBC in JSP:

- JDBC provides a standard API to connect and execute SQL queries on a database.
- Servlets use JDBC to fetch, insert, update, or delete data in the database.

2. Basic Workflow:

- Database Connection: Establish a connection using DriverManager.getConnection().

- SQL Execution: Use PreparedStatement or Statement to execute queries.
- Result Handling: Process the ResultSet for query results.

Example1:-Write a JSP program to display the details of College (CollegeID, Coll_Name, Address) in tabular form on browser.

```
<%@page import="java.sql.*" contentType="text/html"
pageEncoding="UTF-8" %>
<html>
<body>
<%! int hno;
String hname,address;
%>
<% try
{
Class.forName("oracle.jdbc.driver.OracleDriver");
Connection
con=DriverManager.getConnection("jdbc:oracle:thin:@localhost:1521:xe",
"system","root");
Statement st=con.createStatement();
ResultSet rs=st.executeQuery("select * from college"); %>
<table border="1" width="40%">
<tr>
<td>Hospital No</td>
<td>Name</td>
<td>Address</td>
</tr>
<% while(rs.next()) { %>
<tr>
<td>
<%= rs.getInt("cid") %>
</td>
<td>
<%= rs.getString("cname") %>
</td>
<td>
<%= rs.getString("addr") %>
</td>
```

```
</tr>
<%
}
con.close();
}
catch(Exception e){
out.println(e);
}
%>
</body>
</html>
```

Example2:Write a JSP program to accept the details of Account (ANo, Type, Bal) and

store it into database and display it in tabular form.

```
//account.html
<html>
<head>
<meta charset="UTF-8">
<title>Account Details</title>
</head>
<body>
<h1>Account Details</h1>
<form method="post" action="slip22Q1b.jsp">
Account Number: <input type="text" name="accountNumber" /><br>
Account Type: <input type="tcxt" namc="accountTypc" /><br>
Balance: <input type="text" name="balance" /><br>
<input type="submit" value="Add Account" />
</form>
</body>
</html>
//AccountStore.jsp
<%@ page import="java.sql.*" %>
<%! int hno;
String hname,address;
%>
<% try
{
// Establishing Connection
```

```
Class.forName("oracle.jdbc.driver.OracleDriver");
Connection
con=DriverManager.getConnection("jdbc:oracle:thin:@localhost:1521:xe",
"system","root");
Statement st=con.createStatement();
// Query to insert data in Account table
String accountNumber = request.getParameter("accountNumber");
String accountType = request.getParameter("accountType");
int balance = Integer.parseInt(request.getParameter("balance"));
String sql = "INSERT INTO account (accountNumber, accountType,
balance) VALUES (?, ?, ?)";
PreparedStatement statement = con.prepareStatement(sql);
statement.setString(1, accountNumber);
statement.setString(2, accountType);
statement.setInt(3, balance);
int rowsInserted = statement.executeUpdate();
statement.close();
if (rowsInserted > 0) {
out.println("Account added successfully.");
} else {
out.println("Failed to add account.");
}
// Query to fetch all details from account table
ResultSet rs=st.executeQuery("select * from account");
%>
<h2>Accounts</h2>
<table border="1" width="40%">
<tr>
<td>Account No</td>
<td>Type</td>
<td>Balance</td>
</tr>
<%
while(rs.next()) {
out.println("<tr><td>");
out.println(rs.getString(1));
out.println("</td>");
out.println("<td>");
```

```
out.println(rs.getString(2));
out.println("</td>");
out.println("<td>");
out.println(rs.getInt(3));
out.println("</td>");
out.println("</tr>");
}
con.close();
}
catch(Exception e){
out.println(e);
}
%>
</body>
</html>
```

JavaBean

A JavaBean is a Java class that should follow the following conventions:

It should have a no-arg constructor.

It should be Serializable.

It should provide methods to set and get the values of the properties, known as getter and setter methods.

Why use JavaBean?

According to Java white paper, it is a reusable software component. A bean encapsulates many objects into one object so that we can access this object from multiple places. Moreover, it provides easy maintenance.

Simple example of JavaBean class

```
//Employee.java
public class Employee implements java.io.Serializable{
private int id;
private String name;
public Employee(){}
public void setId(int id){this.id=id;}
public int getId(){return id;}
public void setName(String name){this.name=name;}
public String getName(){return name;}
}
```

How to access the JavaBean class?

To access the JavaBean class, we should use getter and setter methods.

```
public class Test{
public static void main(String args[]){
Employee e=new Employee();//object is created
e.setName("Arjun");//setting value to the object
System.out.println(e.getName());
}
}
```

JavaBean Properties

A JavaBean property is a named feature that can be accessed by the user of the object. The feature can be of any Java data type, containing the classes that you define.

A JavaBean property may be read, write, read-only, or write-only. JavaBean features are accessed through two methods in the JavaBean's implementation class:

1. getPropertyName ()

For example, if the property name is firstName, the method name would be getFirstName() to read that property. This method is called the accessor.

2. setPropertyName ()

For example, if the property name is firstName, the method name would be setFirstName() to write that property. This method is called the mutator.

Advantages of JavaBean

The following are the advantages of JavaBean:/p>

The JavaBean properties and methods can be exposed to another application.

It provides an easiness to reuse the software components.

Disadvantages of JavaBean

The following are the disadvantages of JavaBean:

JavaBeans are mutable. So, it can't take advantages of immutable objects.

Creating the setter and getter method for each property separately may lead to the boilerplate code.

Jar files in Java

A JAR (Java Archive) is a package file format typically used to aggregate many Java class files and associated metadata and resources (text, images, etc.) into one file to distribute application software or libraries on the Java platform.

In simple words, a JAR file is a file that contains compressed version of .class files, audio files, image files or directories. We can imagine a .jar files as a zipped file(.zip) that is created by using WinZip software. Even , WinZip software can be used to used to extract the contents of a .jar . So you can use them for tasks such as lossless data compression, archiving, decompression, and archive unpacking.

Let us see how to create a .jar file and related commands which help us to work with .jar files

Create a JAR file: To create a .jar file , we can use jar cf command in the following way:

jar cf jarfilename inputfiles

Here, cf represents create the file. For example , assuming our package pack is available in C:\directory , to convert it into a jar file into the pack.jar , we can give the command as:

C:\> jar cf pack.jar pack

Now , pack.jar file is created.

www.ingramcontent.com/pod-product-compliance
Lightning Source LLC
LaVergne TN
LVHW090131160826
845673LV00017B/2082

* 9 7 9 8 8 9 6 9 9 8 0 2 0 *